POSITIVE
PERFORMANCE
IMPROVEMENT

POSITIVE
PERFORMANCE
IMPROVEMENT

A New Paradigm for
Optimizing Your Workforce

Richard F. Gerson
Robbie G. Gerson

DAVIES-BLACK PUBLISHING
MOUNTAIN VIEW, CALIFORNIA

Published by Davies-Black Publishing, a division of CPP, Inc., 1055 Joaquin Road, 2nd Floor, Mountain View, CA 94043; 800-624-1765.

Special discounts on bulk quantities of Davies-Black books are available to corporations, professional associations, and other organizations. For details, contact the Director of Marketing and Sales at Davies-Black Publishing; 650-691-9123; fax 650-623-9271.

Visit the Davies-Black Publishing Web site at www.daviesblack.com.

10 09 08 07 06   10 9 8 7 6 5 4 3 2 1
Printed in the United States of America

Library of Congress Cataloging-in-Publication Data

Gerson, Richard F.
    Positive performance improvement : a new paradigm for optimizing your workforce /
        Richard F. Gerson and Robbie G. Gerson.—1st ed.
        p. cm.
    Includes index.
    ISBN-13: 978-0-89106-203-5 (hardcover)
    ISBN-10: 0-89106-203-3 (hardcover)
    1. Organizational effectiveness. 2. Performance. I. Gerson, Robbie G. II. Title.
    HD58.9.G48 2006
    658.3'128—dc22

                              2005030093

FIRST EDITION
First printing 2006

CONTENTS

PREFACE

This book has been thirty years in the making. It is both a labor of love and a labor of necessity. Actually, it is not a labor at all, since we truly enjoyed writing it. It came about from our ongoing work with corporate clients who were looking for a better way to improve organizational effectiveness, individual coaching clients who wanted to "get better faster," and teams (sports, business, academic) that wanted a different approach to help them achieve their goals. The book is heavily influenced by our individual areas of expertise as well as their overlap in specific areas. Richard has a background in sport psychology, which is even now morphing into performance psychology. His work in the areas of motivation, performance enhancement techniques, and coaching play a big part in the development and implementation of many aspects of the Positive CORE model. Robbie's background is in human resources, where she has helped many employers and clients develop leaders, maximize talent, and become more effective. The areas of overlap for us include performance improvement, performance management, and people management. This book combines all that and more to provide you with a new approach to help people and organizations be their best.

Another reason we wrote the book is to cut through all the disparate and divergent information that is out there telling people how to achieve high performance—complicated algorithms, warring strategies, and wide-ranging recommendations. This book pulls from accepted areas of positive psychology, strengths psychology, appreciative inquiry, sport psychology, people performance management, and motivational psychology to create an approach that anyone can use to enhance performance. When you use the techniques and model described in this book, you will get the desired results. The book is written for you from the perspective of your role as a manager, needing to know what to do and how to do it. The book gives you a road map to accomplish that.

Furthermore, for this book we have broken with much of the current work in performance improvement. Writers in this field tend to focus on a deficiency perspective: identify a weakness or gap in performance, go through a series of analyses to find out what is wrong and why, and then create an intervention to improve or eliminate the weakness. This is very similar to the current approach in psychology and medicine, both of which look for what is wrong with the patient instead of what is right. We prefer to look for what is right with the performers we work with, where their strengths are, and what we can do to increase those strengths.

STRUCTURE OF THE BOOK

The book is divided into eight chapters. The first three provide a foundation for the model we call Positive CORE (Confidence, Outcomes, Relationships, and Engagement). The next four chapters describe each element of the model, and the final chapter gives you real-world examples of how Positive CORE was implemented and how effective it was for clients.

Chapter 1 describes the psychology of performance improvement, with an emphasis on the people aspects. Much of the literature today in performance improvement focuses on systems, processes, and mechanistic models. Not enough attention is paid to the individual performers and their goals and motivations, and to approaches that can help or hinder individual performance. We prefer to emphasize the importance of the performer in the performance mix. Intuitively obvious as this may seem, the performer is sometimes actually left out of improvement efforts.

Chapter 2 provides you with what we call the central idea for performance enhancement: emotions and other "people factors." It introduces the concepts of how emotions affect performance, how what the performer brings to the table affects performance, and how focusing on the people side rather than the procedural side can have a lasting effect on performance improvement.

Chapter 3 introduces you to the Positive CORE model. It describes each of the four elements in detail, along with the three subcategories for each element, a total of twelve categories in all. These categories, listed below, are interdependent when it comes to ensuring performance enhancement and improvement.

- **Confidence:** Self-esteem, strengths and talents, and reinforcements and consequences
- **Outcomes:** Goals, expectations, and reinforcements; measurement and evaluation; and results as they pertain to individuals, organizations, and society
- **Relationships:** With the manager; with friends and family; and with social, professional, and community contacts
- **Engagement:** Commitment; emotions; and motivation and optimism

Subsequent chapters provide a rationale for each element of the model and how it enhances performance.

Chapter 4 not only tells you what confidence is and how it affects performance but also shows you how to build it up in your people. The chapter makes a case for identifying people's strengths instead of their weaknesses and shows how working with those strengths leads to enhanced self-esteem and increased confidence. An ongoing belief in oneself (confidence) is central to a person's ability to perform well.

Chapter 5 talks about outcomes, which include results, returns, and reinforcements. It explores the seven myths and truths of performance improvement, illustrates how failure can be a positive force, and explains why various types of praise lead to better performance. The chapter also introduces the concept of a performance scoreboard, which makes results visible to the performer.

Chapter 6 describes the importance of various types of relationships and how they can help or hinder performance. One thing that influenced us here is the Gallup information on how employees stay with or leave a company because of their relationship with their manager, and how having a "best friend" at work helps people perform better.

The hot topic of engagement is the focus of Chapter 7. People have to be involved in what they do. They must be motivated and fully engaged to be highly effective and successful. You don't want your people just going through the motions, and this chapter helps you make sure they are engaged, involved, and in control. This chapter also introduces a mini-model of a tool we use called TOPS: Talent Optimization Performance System. TOPS takes the Positive CORE strategy and shows how to make it tactical and practical. Additionally, TOPS can be used for coaching, performance appraisal, and ongoing performance management.

Chapter 8 brings the entire book together. It describes how to use the Positive CORE model in its entirety. The bulk of the book describes the model itself, with some stories about how the model was used. These descriptions are very general. This chapter breaks down the process into its three phases: interview, coaching, and implementation. It provides examples of the kinds of questions to use during the interview phase, then shows you how to evaluate the results of the interviews and develop a plan for performance enhancement. Finally, it lays out what you need to know to implement your plan. The chapter concludes with several real-world examples from sales, health care, and sports.

OUR CHALLENGE TO YOU

Each chapter of the book ends with a section called "Our Challenge to You." This section asks you and challenges you to do something positive with what you've learned in the chapter. Some chapters ask you to take what you've learned and apply it immediately; others challenge you to make some changes in your organization. In any case, the idea is for you to create positive change wherever you are and to make a positive impact that adds value. So, at this time, our challenge to you is to read this book with an open mind, think about how you feel moving from a negative perspective to a more positive approach to performance improvement, and consider what you can do to enhance what we describe in the book. We would love to hear from you about how you implement the Positive CORE approach and the TOPS model and the results you are getting. You can reach us at getrich@richgerson.com or robbie.gerson@richgerson.com.

Richard F. Gerson
Robbie G. Gerson
Clearwater, Florida

ACKNOWLEDGMENTS

Some of our friends and colleagues have influenced our writing of this book. Roger Kaufman, one of the founders of what is now called the International Society for Performance Improvement (ISPI), who has as one of his major goals in life to help people achieve perfect performance, tells us and everyone else to make sure that whatever we do has a positive impact and adds value to society. When you follow the models and principles in this book, you will definitely achieve positive results, maximize performance, and add value for whomever you are working with. Dale Brethower says if you care, get the facts. Because we care, the material in this book is based largely on facts derived from our own experiences plus the research and published theories of other experts.

It was our choice to write this book as an easier read than if it were a research report or textbook. Rest assured that everything in here is based on accepted theory and facts. Plus, we made sure that we integrated, synthesized, and coordinated those facts in creating the Positive CORE model and the other recommendations in the book. Jay Jamrog, of the Human Resources Institute, is constantly talking about moving human resources to a more positive, strategic approach based on people performance management. He, like us, continuously advocates for finding people's strengths and helping them maximize those strengths to their own and their organization's benefit. Dick Nimphie, a good friend and client, is the Executive General Manager at Lexus of Tampa Bay, Florida. He has been and is a role model for the Positive CORE concepts. His people love him and constantly set sales records because he focuses on their strengths. We truly want to thank these friends and colleagues for their insight, recommendations, influence, and, most of all, friendship.

We also want to acknowledge several other people in the writing of this book. We begin with Roger Chevalier of ISPI. Roger believed in this book and spearheaded the effort to get it published. Despite numerous other responsibilities for ISPI, he forged ahead and arranged for Davies-Black to publish the book. Which leads us to Connie Kallback, our editor. Connie is the consummate professional and the best editor any author can hope to work with. She asked a great deal of us and she gave a great deal in return. We also want to thank the team at Davies-Black who took things to another level to get this book published in such a short period of time. Everyone worked in "sixth gear" to produce the book, and we want to thank them profusely.

Thank you also to our friends, colleagues, and teachers (through the years) who have influenced and challenged our thinking. While too numerous to mention individually, you all know who you are. We also owe a debt of gratitude to our clients, both organizational and individual. It was through working with them that we were able to develop and test the principles of the Positive CORE model and refine it to where it is today.

Plus, we want to thank our sons, Michael and Mitchell. They indulged us as we wrote this book. They also have been willing and unwilling "guinea pigs" for us as we tested the principles of the model on them and on their friends and teammates. That is one reason that, in addition to our client work, we know the model works in business, sports, and academia.

And finally, we want to thank each other. Working together is one thing, and writing a book is another. It takes a tremendous amount of understanding and effort, and it takes your relationship to greater depths and higher levels. This effort has definitely helped us strengthen our CORE, even after twenty-five years of marriage.

ABOUT THE AUTHORS

Richard Gerson is president of Gerson Goodson, Inc., a consulting firm specializing in helping people and organizations be their best and increase their effectiveness through the use of research-based performance psychology techniques. The company works with clients in the areas of leadership development, talent optimization, performance management, sales, and marketing.

Richard was one of the pioneers in the performance psychology field, having developed training programs and consulting services in this area since 1979. He is an expert in identifying behavioral and mental strategies that people use to perform at a high level and then developing training programs to both improve the performance of the exemplars and transfer those strategies to other performers. Richard's strength in helping others achieve high levels of performance and success lies in his abilities to coach and mentor people in such a way that they expand their comfort zones, stretch their limits, and turn the stresses of their lives into the successes of their lives. He uses a variety of techniques from sport and performance psychology, cognitive-behavioral psychology, and neurolinguistic psychology to accomplish these goals. He also helps salespeople, athletes, executives, and students train their brains to perform more effectively and successfully.

Richard has a Ph.D. in sport psychology from Florida State University. He has published nineteen books and more than four hundred articles in journals, magazines, newspapers, and newsletters. He is a certified performance technologist, a certified management consultant, a certified professional marketing consultant, and the holder of several other professional certifications. He was recently given a lifetime achievement award by the Tampa Bay chapter of the International Society for Performance Improvement. He is a past president of that chapter.

Robbie G. Gerson is executive vice president and managing partner of Gerson Goodson, Inc. She holds a master's degree in leadership and organizational effectiveness and has twenty years' experience in human resources and performance management. Her expertise in the selection and hiring of top talent has helped her former employers and current clients realize significant gains in productivity and performance. Robbie has been coaching executives and leaders to help them achieve their full potential and also to enable them to empower their employees to reach their potential. Using the techniques in the Gerson Goodson performance improvement book, she helps clients attain measurable results, improve organizational effectiveness, and build better relationships within their organizations and with their clients. She also focuses on leadership development, talent optimization, and performance management.

PSYCHOLOGY OF PERFORMANCE IMPROVEMENT

A Focus on People

Why does performance improvement consulting fail so often? Here's an example:

VCI operated a call center to handle customer service issues for a cable television company. The customer service representatives all went through the same training program, which focused on computer and software operation, product and programming knowledge, customer service skills, and communication skills. Nevertheless, only 10 percent of the reps were achieving specified goals. The other 90 percent were exhibiting inferior performance. So VCI contacted a consultant to develop training programs to improve the performance of the majority of the reps.

The consultant convinced VCI that training might not be the answer and that she should be allowed to use her expertise and what she called "human performance technology" (HPT) skills to determine the exact nature of the performance problem and how to solve it. VCI agreed and the consultant used a gap analysis model to identify the problem and select an appropriate solution. She employed her HPT education and training to determine a performance improvement (PI) intervention, which involved changing some of the procedures in the call center.

VCI followed the consultant's recommendations and implemented the new procedures. To everyone's surprise and disappointment, performance did not improve. Changes had been made, yet the results were not achieved. That's when the consultant called on us for help. She wanted to know what she had missed or done wrong.

What do you think was left out of the performance improvement equation that caused the intervention to "fail"?

THE WRONG FOCUS

These days, performance improvement efforts all seem to focus on the same things: the policies, processes, and procedures of the organization or company, and the models, systems, and flow charts to be used to change those policies, processes, and procedures when they are not working properly. Current writers on the subject would have you believe that employees will improve their performance within the organization as long as the prescribed performance intervention is followed and the company's goals and the individual's goals and skill sets are aligned. Yet with all this advice, and with all the advances in human and electronic performance technology, few companies are getting the results they want and expect.

That is because the focus of most recent performance improvement publications, efforts, and interventions is wrong. Many articles, reports, and books talk about the technology of PI (its models, systems, and flow charts), the integration of a PI approach with a company's current productivity processes, and the training required to get performers up to speed. Similar publications, such as those in the knowledge management and human resources area, discuss how important it is to "capture" all the performers' knowledge and information so that others will benefit from their "expertise." Then, by somehow transferring this expertise, performance will improve.

This is the wrong focus.

It is too centered on the company that is using the human performance technology. With this approach, no company can ever tell if it has too much technology (which means too many models or system changes), too little technology, or just enough. Its leaders will also never know whether the intervention they selected truly had a positive effect on future performance because they are leaving out the most important part of the equation.

GUARANTEEING PERFORMANCE IMPROVEMENT

There is only one way to guarantee performance improvement and to make sure individuals move from ordinary performance to extraordinary performance. To do this, you must push the performance technology aspects to the background and place your focus squarely on the "object of your affections": the performer. That is, spend more time with the *human* portion of the human performance technology equation. After all, what good is a technologically enhanced and advanced, front end–analyzed, needs-assessed view of performance if the performers

- Don't want us to know why they do what they do?

- Don't want to give up the information they have acquired?

- Want to totally control the aspects and closeness of the performance "relationship," and really do not want management that close?

That is why it's essential to focus on each performer and what that performer wants from us. An effective way to build a truly high-performing organization using human performance technology is to pay attention to each performer's *memories, emotions, motivations,* and *experiences* (terms we use as the basis for a handy acronym: MEME).

You may be wondering why we picked four things to consider that spell out *meme.* A meme is an idea that spreads or reproduces much like a gene or even a virus. Most memes are good ideas, and people benefit when they learn about them. Our selection of the acronym MEME is to help you remember the four items and to motivate you to "spread the word" that this often-neglected aspect of HPT is really the key to success.

Another reason we selected the acronym MEME is to help you remember how these four elements affect the psychology of performers and their performance improvement efforts. You will notice throughout the book that we've used acronyms and abbreviations (such as HPT and PI for "human performance technology" and "performance improvement") to help you more easily remember the terms and what they stand for. These abbreviations are standard fare in the performance field, so learning, understanding, and using them will help you become part of the "in crowd."

THE MEME OF HPT

HPT is definitely an idea whose time has come. From the performer's perspective, it can be a boon or a bust. Applied properly, HPT helps you learn about the performer you are trying to help. Whatever you know about your performer usually helps you move your relationship along in a positive manner so that performance improves. Sometimes, however, too much knowledge about the performer can get you in hot water because you begin playing on "personal matters" to motivate the performer to achieve. This brings us to *memories,* the first item in the new psychology of HPT and PI.

MEMORIES

People's performance levels within your business will be built in part on the memories they have of their work with you. If those memories are positive, people will likely seek you out for continued enjoyable encounters. If those memories are negative due to poor treatment, unmet expectations, or rude behavior, you have virtually no chance of developing a top performer.

While many companies strive to get performers to *think* positively, you should take a different approach. Work to get performers to *remember* positive things about you and their previous successful performances. Consistently recalled positive memories are a stronger influence on future decision making and performance than are any number of new messages about performance improvement because your target must first become aware of, then attend to, and then accept each new message. Recalled positive memories bubble up to the surface instantly and immediately put the performer in the proper frame of mind for the next action.

For example, let's say one of your people is having trouble meeting production deadlines. You have tried a variety of approaches but nothing seems to work. At this point, many managers might threaten to fire the person. That won't work, either; something is holding this person back from being more productive, and the threat won't make it go away. What you should do is ask about past efforts, either on the job or in another activity, when a deadline did get met. Then, get the person to visualize the successful performance, recall the pleasant memories from that situation, and transfer those memories and their associated behaviors to the current situation.

Use this positive memory approach with current production deadlines and you'll be pleasantly surprised by the results.

EMOTIONS

Why is it that every person and company seems to talk about the importance of emotions, but no one really pays attention to them? Leaders promote the skills of empathy and compassion, talk about training people in emotional intelligence, and even tell performers how much they care about them and how much they should care about others. Yet most people really pay little attention to how performers feel and how those emotions affect their performance.

As you know, emotions are a fickle business. Much has been written about them, including their effect on mood, performance, and human interaction. Yet, with all the support for the influence of emotions on a performer's psyche and psychology, few people pay enough attention to them.

When was the last time you asked any of your performers how they felt and truly listened to their answers? When did you spend enough time with anyone to understand how he or she responds in specific situations and then place that information in your HPT system so everyone will know the emotional profile of the performer? And how well do you truly understand that what performers need psychologically is often more important than what they need from a business perspective?

Understanding the emotions of your performers is critical to your success and the success of your HPT/PI initiative.

It is often said that performers in business are like athletes. Everyone expects them to perform at a high level regardless of the situation. Yet, in sports, coaches and fans focus on and talk about the athletes' emotions before and during every event. Athletes are said to be up or down for a game. What may have caused them to feel this way is endlessly interesting, as are ways to get them in a positive mood so they will feel better and ultimately perform better.

Yet business hardly ever takes this approach. Why? What's holding business back from realizing that the emotions of the performer are an important part of business achievement and success? Think about how well or how poorly you performed on a given day or in a given situation. Now, assess your emotional state at the time of the performance and relate it to the outcome. There is a definite relationship here, and you must find that relationship in the people whose performances you are helping improve. Emotions are critical to success.

MOTIVATIONS

Many things can motivate people: money, love, fear, recognition, sex, achievement, ego, and a host of other factors. Motivations are closely tied to emotions. So we ask you, what do you truly know about what motivates your performers?

Why did they come to work for you in the first place? What motivated them to make the decision to change their status quo, and to change it with you? How can your knowledge of your performers' motivations help you build relationships with them that will lead to ongoing high performance? And how will this information help you work with the performers to make them better performers?

Motivation is what drives all of us. It gets us up in the morning, off to work or play, and home again. Motivation determines why we enter into relationships, with whom, and how well we do in those relationships. Motivation is often the hidden key factor when a performer achieves extraordinary results. This is the way things work in the real world.

We strongly recommend that you focus your HPT/PI efforts on understanding the motivations of your performers, not just how and when they do their jobs and how much you can get them to do. By paying more attention to their motivations for their performance behaviors, you will be able to generate higher levels of productivity and profitability.

Now, we're not suggesting you go right out and study everything you can on motivation (and its cousin, performance incentives). If you keep the following three points in mind, you will be able to increase the motivation levels of your performers, which will result in better performance. Remember that all performers

1. Must motivate themselves internally

2. Crave external rewards, even though these work for only a short while

3. Are motivated by achievement, power, friendship, recognition, and love

Keep these concepts in mind and you'll be able to help your people increase their motivation to achieve higher levels of performance.

EXPERIENCES

Without doubt, this is an experience economy. Anyone involved in customer service now knows that it is the total customer experience, not just what happens at the point of sale or complaint resolution, that determines how truly satisfied customers are with what you provide for them and how loyal they will be.

Similarly, performers in your organization judge you by the experience they have when they work for you or interact with you. You work hard to train your people to be the best performers possible. You give them opportunities to show that they are capable performers and you evaluate their performances. What you probably fail to do is ask performers how *they* perceived and interpreted the experience. Unfortunately, that reaction is quite often more important than how you perceived and interpreted their experience during their performance.

Now, we're not talking about performer surveys. You wouldn't send a survey to your best friend, Karen, to ask her how she liked something you did for her. Rather, you would bring it up in conversation. And Karen's answers would determine how you would structure the next experience you had together.

Similarly, if Karen were to buy something from you, you would ask her directly how she liked the entire purchase experience. Again, you would ask and listen as she described the good, the bad, and the ugly (or maybe all the good). What you would not do is send her a survey. We're not knocking surveys here. We are simply suggesting that for you to truly understand your friend's experience, the two of you have to talk.

The point is you must engage people in dialogue about the experience of work and productivity. You must ask performers to help you improve the experience in the future. You must get at their psychological interpretation of the experience (hoping it is positive but prepared to hear and work on any negative aspects) if you want them to develop into high performers.

SPREADING THE MEME

As we said earlier, a meme is like a gene or virus that spreads or reproduces. In this case, you must first use the MEME acronym to help you train your mind as to what will help your people become better performers. Then, you can help your performers establish and recall positive memories, positive emotions, appropriate motivations, and positive experiences related to their particular performances.

The success of your HPT/PI effort depends on how well you know your performers. You must understand the psychology behind their behaviors. You must learn how they think, how they compare your past behaviors with your present ones (memories), how they feel about working with and for you (emotions), what drives them to work for you or someone else (motivations), and how they interpret each encounter with you (experiences). When you know these things, you can turn your HPT system into a technologically advanced, human-focused, continuous performance improvement effort.

More important, when you know these things about your performers, you can spread the MEME and develop a very competent performer base.

THE PSYCHOLOGICAL SIDE

Programs like TQM, business process reengineering, downsizing, and quality circles never seem to live up to their billing. The management fad of the day is as ineffective as the diet fad of the week. If either worked well, you would not see so many new fads creeping into the marketplace.

On the other hand, performance consultants, coaches, and technologists have great difficulty convincing human resource directors, CEOs, and laypeople of the benefits of their work. Is it because they do not have quantifiable results that they can point to? Or is it because as a field of study, HPT is too theoretical and process and model oriented?

For us, it is the latter reason. HPT professionals do an excellent job of analyzing performance problems and proposing workable solutions. They also do an excellent job of implementing those solutions when given the chance. So why is it so hard to win people over? And why is it so difficult to get the ultimate results that people want to see with regard to their performances?

The reason is that, while HPT theories, models, and assumptions are technically sound, they are rarely people oriented. They are usually process, system, or organization oriented instead. It is important for HPT as a field of inquiry to take into account both the technological side of performance improvement and the emotional side of it; only then will it have a chance to achieve high-level results on a consistent basis.

When people engage in a work-related activity, they bring to it a mind-set, a set of behaviors, beliefs, and values, and a heart full of emotions. Performance improvement efforts must influence all of these factors. It does not matter how good your theories and processes are if you forget about the performers behind the performance.

It's also necessary to include the performers' psychological approach to taking action: their levels of self-confidence and self-esteem, how they deal with stress, how well they perform under pressure, if they set goals, their expectations of success, their intrinsic reward system, and what motivates them to achieve. If you really want to upgrade people's performances using HPT, focus heavily on the psychology of performance improvement.

This idea is really not new, as it was suggested decades ago by Drucker, Maslow, and others. These experts said that in order to improve performance, you must treat individuals in a way that accounts for their intrinsic motivations, belief and behavior systems, and perceptions of the impact of their performances. This sounds like the same message: pay more attention to the psychology of performance improvement in order to get real change.

THE MENTAL STATE OF THE PERFORMER

Performers enter performance situations in specific mental states. Some are positive, some are neutral, some are negative, and some just don't have a clue. Their mental state definitely affects how well they perform and whether they achieve their performance goals. Performers who are self-confident and believe in their abilities do well on their tasks more often than those who are not self-confident or who doubt their abilities.

Think of articles about your favorite sports team in your local newspaper. More often than not, you will find references by the coaches and the players to the mental state of the athletes. They will say things like "we won because we were mentally prepared," or "we lost because we were not mentally ready (or mentally tough)." The same concepts hold true on the job. Many times, employees make mistakes because they are not paying attention (not being mentally prepared or focused) or are not motivated to complete the task. This is an important point for companies to take into account. The mental readiness and attitudes of their employees will affect those employees' performances, for better or worse.

A positive attitude and a high level of self-esteem are essential to superior performances. A performer who has already experienced success in past activities will enter into new performance situations expecting to succeed again. High perceived expectations of success result in significant performance improvements over past efforts as well as higher levels of achievement on repetitive tasks. And since many work tasks are repetitive, you now have one of the psychological secrets to guaranteeing performance improvement: Make sure employees are successful on specific tasks, help them generate positive expectations related to success on future tasks, and then challenge them to meet or exceed the current achievement level.

Here is another secret to guaranteeing performance improvement: When these factors combine with a task that is matched to the person's abilities and is inherently challenging (which in goal-setting terms we call hard but obtainable), the performer often enters into a flow state. You know what a flow state is. It's when everything happens naturally and very easily. You don't even have to think about what you are doing. Executives talk about it during brainstorming sessions. Salespeople call it being "in the zone" when they easily make one sale after another. Athletes also talk about being in the zone. The common element here is that they are all in a flow state, and that produces a peak performance.

It is up to performance technologists to take these factors into account because they affect the performers' mental state. Consider the performers' self-esteem, their expectations for success, how they perceive their task in relation to their current skill set, and how well they have done on related tasks in the past. One way to help performers achieve a positive mental state is to praise and reinforce both their successful behaviors and their successful approximations of the desired behaviors. Such praise improves the likelihood that desirable behaviors will be repeated and the intrinsic motivation of the performers will increase.

Another aspect of the performers' mental state to consider is the way performers respond to and perform under stress. We discuss the effects of stress on performance in greater detail later in the chapter. For now, realize that stress has a major effect on performance improvements and outcomes. Stress is normally regarded as hindering performance—by increasing anxiety, nervousness, and tension. You must teach people how to relax and perform under pressure if you want to realize high-level performance results. People who can make themselves relax find that stress becomes a challenge, a motivator, and an ally. It helps them get into the act of successfully completing their task.

Do you know people who cannot write a report or a term paper until the night before it is due? Haven't you wondered how they deal with all that pressure, when they could avoid it by being sensible and starting much sooner? These people are thrill seekers of a sort, and they thrive on the pressure of deadlines. Pressure and stress motivate them and challenge them. They get themselves into the zone only when they are under stress. If you identify any of your employees as top performers under stress, work with them to create challenging situations. You will be amazed and delighted by their responses.

MASTERING THE PSYCHOLOGY OF PI

It is generally accepted that the mind plays an important part in everything people do. Then why do so many organizations spend so much time, effort, and money on systems, technology, and instructional media when they try to improve performance but only give lip service to the role psychology plays in performance? Pouring information into performers does not guarantee that they will respond in a positive manner to improvement overtures. In fact, there is a greater likelihood that they will not respond because their psyche was not considered in this mechanistic approach.

Performers must see PI as something that is intrinsically rewarding; they must receive self-satisfaction from getting better at whatever they are doing if they are to remain intrinsically motivated to repeat the task again and again.

Many people promote the behavioristic approach to PI. For them, every time someone does something right, you give him or her an external reward for positive reinforcement. Then that person will be motivated to repeat the behavior under the premise that what gets rewarded gets repeated.

Generally, however, continually providing external rewards (such as money, prizes, or the like) every time a performer approximates an improvement or achieves a performance goal runs the risk of eventually causing a loss of intrinsic motivation for that task. For some reason, when people receive intangible rewards—praise, recognition, or appreciation for what they have accomplished—they become more motivated to perform again. Maybe it has something to do with how their minds process the reinforcement.

Salespeople who get financial incentives for achieving certain quotas seem to raise their performances early on after receiving the rewards. After a while, their sales either stagnate or drop back to pre-reward levels. While many believe this physical or financial reward system works for everyone, in truth it works more often for pigeons and for rats in a maze than it does for people. If people do not perceive a real gain from the performance—psychological, emotional, or physical (and sometimes financial)—then that "desired behavior" will not be repeated, regardless of the reward or reinforcement.

The behaviorist approach often leaves out the cognitive, or thought, processes of the performer. But people are always thinking about what they are doing. And those thoughts lead to emotions, which become attached to the performance. Sometimes the emotions come before the thoughts, but the attachment still occurs. This is why it is essential to pay attention to both the mental state and the emotions of the performer when you are trying to bring about performance improvement.

Another area where HPT technologists tend to be remiss involves either negating or forgetting about the roles commitment, desire, and passion play in performance improvement. Yes, these are types of emotions, and yes, they do have an effect on performance. But remember that all learning, memory recall, and performance occur best when the current situation approximates the previous performance situation. This means that not only must the environment be similar, but the emotional and mental states of the performer also must be similar.

It's human nature: If we are highly aroused when we learn a new way to perform an old task (performance improvement), or even when we learn a new task, then we must also be highly aroused when we are expected to perform that task in a different real-world situation. If we have a passion for doing something, we must exhibit that passion every time if we want to consistently achieve a high level of performance. Conversely, when we are not committed to or passionate about something, we either do not do it at all or we just go through the motions without the necessary emotions. The end result is that we do not perform well.

How many times have you done everything exactly according to the HPT model—you completed your needs assessment and front-end analysis, identified your performance gaps, identified and developed the appropriate intervention, created the proper performance aids that would lead to performance improvement, implemented the intervention—and then watched it fall flat on its face? What was missing?

What was missing was the person. Again, the problem human performance technologists run into is that they focus too much on the technology (systems) and not enough on the person (human). It's necessary to spend more time on the people side of every model. When you do this, you will master the psychology of PI.

WHAT MAKES PEOPLE TICK?

This question has been bothering practitioners for decades. Numerous attempts have been made to find out what makes people tick and how to motivate them. People have been scientifically managed, managed by objectives, downsized, reengineered, delayered, placed in teams and quality circles, CBT'ed (computer-based training), WBL'ed (Web-based learning), and who knows what else. They have been financially rewarded, travel rewarded, promotion rewarded, and on and on. And the outcome of all these efforts has been less than stellar. Why? They all forget about two things: the people involved and their psyches.

Here is the best way to find out what makes people tick: *ASK*. "ASK" is an acronym for "always seek knowledge," which serves as a reminder that you will find out what moves people by asking them. Learn what they are passionate about. Learn what gets them out of bed in the morning. Learn why they drag themselves through the day at work and then find enormous amounts of energy to do volunteer work, play golf, participate in a book group, or anything else afterward. Find out what creates the fire in their belly and what they are truly passionate about. Discover how and why they create peak performances in so many areas of their lives, yet not at work. Your goal is to get them to tell you, so you can help them continuously and consistently get better at what they do.

When you learn this, you will know what makes each person tick. Then you can create customized and individualized PI programs so that everyone improves his or her performance over time. You may even get lucky and create the conditions under which your people become highly motivated and consistent peak performers. Now, that would be a nice situation for every organization to have.

You may have to overcome one obstacle, though. Every performance has some stress associated with it, and every performer responds to stress differently. So, in addition to learning what makes people tick, you must learn how they respond to stress.

EFFECTS OF STRESS ON PERFORMANCE

When people know that they are involved in a PI effort, it creates stress for some of them. There are people who respond well to stressful situations, while others react poorly to them. For some, the stress is just right, while for others it is simply too much. When a situation offers too much stress, or even too little, performance suffers. People need just the right amount of stress (what psychologists refer to as being in the optimal arousal zone) to achieve performance changes, improvements, and peak performance.

The simplest way to help performers deal with stress is to teach them two fundamental stress management techniques: relaxation through deep breathing and visualization. When people are able to combine these two techniques prior to a performance situation, they usually can handle any adversity that comes up and achieve a better-than-expected performance. Plus, the performers will feel better about themselves for doing so well while under stress. The result will be increased self-confidence and self-esteem, and an increased desire to engage in the performance again.

You must familiarize yourself with the benefits of visualization (mental imagery). Many great athletes, musicians, dancers, and other performers visualize a performance before actually doing it. In this way, they experience a sort of déjà vu when they actually engage in the performance. If you want to effect significant performance improvements, have the performers rehearse the desired positive behavioral changes in their minds before they go out and perform. You may find that this alone improves results without going through the entire HPT analysis, intervention, and evaluation process.

One of the clichés we hear regarding stress and performance is that it is not how many times you get knocked down but how many times you get up. In effect, you need to get up one time more than you are knocked down. So if your performance improvement efforts are meeting with resistance or are not achieving the levels you expect, ask the performers what is going on inside their heads and hearts. Ask them if they feel they have been knocked down by this latest PI approach and do not know how to get up. If you get a yes answer, you must deal with this psychological issue first. You must give them the tools and the means to handle the stress, to pick themselves up and perform up to your expectations and their own.

The key here is to help people perform under pressure. Top athletes and top salespeople have developed a variety of ways to achieve this ability to do well under stress. There are many techniques, including the top two (relaxation and visualization), as well as positive self-talk, self-hypnosis, and physical walk-throughs of an activity. The more people practice doing a task, the better they will become at doing it. They will also be better able to handle the stress and pressure because they are now more familiar with the task and the expected outcomes.

FOCUSING ON THE PERFORMER

In our work with corporations and individuals (athletes, business executives, salespeople, students, the general population), we have found a series of protocols, or procedures, that virtually guarantee performance improvement. The reason they work every time is that they focus on the person, not on the technology. These approaches consider the whole performer first before applying the science of PI and HPT. They are all extremely simple to apply.

The first step is to help the performer answer the WIIFM question—What's in it for me? Unless people see and believe in a tangible emotional benefit to improving performance, they will not put forth the necessary effort. You must help each performer understand the relevance of the improvement.

Once relevance is established, you need to determine the performer's set of beliefs. People have two sets of beliefs, those that are enabling and those that are disabling. For improvement to occur, you must identify both sets of beliefs so that you can help the performer overcome the disabling beliefs and establish a strong set of enabling beliefs.

One way to help performers develop enabling beliefs is to teach them to repeat affirmations: positive subvocal statements that motivate, encourage, and enhance the belief system. While some professionals say that affirmations don't really work, and any improvement is only a placebo effect, who cares? If the affirmations increase someone's self-confidence and motivation to perform, then everyone involved with or affected by the performance should be happy. That's why affirmations are an excellent way to build up a performer's belief system.

When the proper belief system has been established, help performers identify the links between their own value systems and the value of the improvement to the organization. Finding the alignment between the performers' personal values and the organization's values motivates the performers to provide their full energies to the improvement effort. If people do not see the value in improving, both to themselves and to the organization, then the effort will be an exercise in futility.

This focus on the performer will also help improve your relationship with that person. There is much evidence that the primary reason employees leave their jobs is a poor relationship with the boss. The opposite is also true. People tend to stay in a position when they have a positive relationship with their boss. So anything you do to learn about your employees and to help them find the relevance in what they do and align their beliefs and values with those of the organization will help you strengthen your relationship with them. And a strong relationship often leads to people wanting to do their best for their boss.

Here is a real-world example from one of our consulting and coaching clients, although the names have been changed.

Lynn was a strong senior-level manager who micromanaged on a regular basis. She had already run off two finance managers in her division and could not see her involvement in their reasons for leaving. She always attributed turnover to a bad hire by human resources. When we began coaching Lynn, we identified her beliefs and values and how they aligned with those of her organization. We worked through any differences and arrived at a mutually agreeable point where she was confident in her beliefs and values, in her ability to communicate them to her staff, and in her alignment with the organization. She was now ready to work with her new finance manager.

Tanya came to the organization highly motivated and ready to take on the world. She had worked with Lynn for two months before Lynn began her coaching with us. In those two months, Tanya's motivation and subsequent performances had dropped. Tanya felt that she was being micromanaged (she was) and that her decisions were always being questioned by Lynn (they were). So, before Lynn could change Tanya, Lynn had to change herself.

We accomplished the change in Lynn and then she set out to catch Tanya doing things right. Lynn was instructed to praise Tanya and show appreciation for her work and accomplishments. Over the next few weeks, their relationship improved and Tanya started to show signs of being highly motivated again. Now it was time for Lynn to talk to Tanya about what they both wanted from their jobs (the WIIFM question), their beliefs, values, alignment, and combined alignment with the organization.

Lynn and Tanya worked things out. They continue to work on their relationship, and Tanya is considered one of the top performers in the entire organization. And it all started because her manager was willing to improve her own performance in order to improve her relationship with one of her people, which eventually led to Tanya's becoming a top performer.

Tanya's high level of performance was a direct result of her improved positive relationship with Lynn. You can be sure that if this relationship had not improved, Tanya would not have become a top performer and she probably would have left the organization. Congratulations are due both Lynn and Tanya for communicating their beliefs, values, and alignment and elevating their performance levels.

GOAL SETTING

Premature goal setting is another obstacle to performance improvement. Upon spotting a performance gap, HPT professionals move right to goal setting to identify what must be done and how it will be done. Yet goals are not appropriate until you take care of three essentials: answering the WIIFM question, establishing enabling beliefs regarding the performance, and aligning values. Only then will the performer be ready to engage in improvement efforts.

You must jointly set goals related to the improvement. You must also establish performance expectations. The performer must know what you expect, and you must know whether the performer believes the improvement is possible, based on the criteria for success and the performance expectations. Even though your needs analysis may have uncovered the improvement goal, you need to get the performer to write down the goal from a personal perspective. The performer must understand the goal in terms of his or her current mind-set, emotions, and mental readiness. Buy-in and belief are the two major factors that will lead to goal achievement here.

Another thing that must be considered is the timing of the improvement effort. Ask if the performer is ready to undertake the effort and able to apply mind, body, and soul to the effort (that is, take part with passion and commitment). If not, why waste your time? Wait until a more appropriate time to start the improvement effort. However, if your situation is such that the improvement must occur now, you may have to bring in outside temporary help to get the job done until the performer is psychologically and emotionally ready.

SEVEN R'S GUARANTEE IMPROVEMENT

We have found that seven elements or factors always lead to performance improvement in business as well as in sports. They are *rapport, respect, response, reinforcement, repetition, rhythm,* and *ritual.*

- **Rapport:** First you must establish rapport with the performer. To engage in performance improvement effectively and successfully, the performer must know that you are on the same team in this improvement effort and feel comfortable with you and the task at hand.

- **Respect:** Next you must respect the performer and communicate that respect. You can show respect in many ways: by acknowledging the performer's efforts, communicating that you appreciate those efforts, and being willing to allow the performer to learn from mistakes.

- **Response:** Following this, you must clearly explain as well as demonstrate the desired response or response set. The performer must know exactly what must be done, how it looks when it is done correctly, and how it feels when it is right.

- **Reinforcement:** When the performer does it correctly, you must reinforce the performance with verbal feedback and praise. This recognition is more intrinsically motivating and therefore longer lasting than tokens or financial incentives.

- **Repetition:** The positive reinforcement will also lead to repetition of the appropriate response (improvement). The more the performer repeats the proper response, the more it becomes ingrained in memory so that future performances can occur at a high level, as if automatically.

- **Rhythm:** If you can create a rhythm to the performance it will be easier for the performer. Everything has a rhythm to it. Help the performer identify the best rhythm associated with the improvement task. Pay attention to the way people move, what they say (often this is an outward display of thought processes), and what they do when the performance is completed. Rhythm helps people do better whatever they do. For example, when you are typing on your keyboard, your fingers get "smarter" and faster when you establish a rhythm to your typing. The same is true when you are giving a speech or business presentation. Your rhythm (sometimes called pacing in these situations) can be the single most important factor in how much people like your presentation.

- **Ritual:** Now sit back and watch the types of rituals the performer creates to complete the new skill. Basketball players bounce the ball several times before shooting a foul shot. Golfers wave the club back and forth before hitting the ball. Dancers use a certain stretching routine before they perform. Businesspeople talk to themselves as they rehearse a presentation. Some people do physical stretching exercises before getting up in front of a group to talk; it helps them relax and focus on the performance. These are all rituals. When performers develop a ritual for a task, you can be sure there will be improvement as well as a high level of achievement because they are repeating a series or pattern of behaviors that they are comfortable with and that have led to successful performances in the past.

PERFORMANCE ATTRIBUTIONS

When people complete a performance, they always make attributions about the reasons for their results. These outcomes are often attributed to the performer's ability, effort, or luck, or to the difficulty of the task. When a performer shows improvement and achieves the performance goal, you want to make sure that the positive experience is attributed to ability. This is called an *internal and stable* attribution and is related to future positive performance expectations and outcomes. If the performer falls short of the performance goal, the outcome should be attributed to either the need for greater effort or the conditions of the task. In this way, the person avoids getting discouraged and instead remains willing to make some changes and try again.

When performers attribute successful task outcomes to luck or an easy task, you have a problem. They feel they had virtually nothing to do with the outcome. The next time the task arises, they will probably lack the motivation to perform. Or, if they do perform, it will be with a half-hearted effort because they do not believe they are in control of the outcome. Understanding a performer's attributions for performance outcomes helps you better focus on the performer as an individual, and it is critical to generating PI. Developing this understanding will be more effective for you in the long run than just throwing money, trips, or other external rewards at your people.

EXTERNAL REWARDS

As we said earlier, external rewards can sometimes decrease the motivation to perform. True as this often is, there is a way to prevent it from happening, and that is why we are revisiting this important topic briefly.

Go directly to the performer and ask what types of rewards would be most welcome as recognition for accomplishing your mutual goals. Take the answer and provide whatever the performer requests. Someone who has decided what reward is motivating will continue to improve performances or at least keep up a high level of performance in the future to maintain a supply of that reward. Here's a real-world example.

Our client could not get managers to compete for a travel reward based on controlling expenses. When we asked the group what they would prefer, they said they wanted the money instead so that they could stay home with their families instead of being alone on an incentive trip.

When the travel perks were converted to financial incentives as pre-scribed by the performers, performance improved.

Reward systems can work, but only if they are developed and imple-mented in conjunction with the performers who will be receiving them. Many managers and organizations, thinking that rewards will create improvements in performance, make the mistake of developing a reward program without including the people actually affected by the rewards— so it should be no surprise that when the rewards and performance goals are announced, the motivation levels of the performers don't seem to increase. Nor do their performance levels.

The secret is to get the performers involved in creating their own rewards. It is quite a challenge to help people become top performers . . . but all great managers and performers love a challenge, so go for it!

OUR CHALLENGE TO YOU

There you have it: a simple yet effective way to improve performance, guaranteed. Start and end with the person. Focus on the psychological issues related to performance improvement rather than the technological issues. Pay attention to motives, beliefs, values, attributions, the ability to perform under stress, performance rituals, affirmations, expectations of success, and the emotional state of the performer. While this may seem like a great deal to focus on, you really cannot avoid it. Most PI efforts that focus on the technology of the field do not achieve the desired results. Only by focusing on the person first, and on the psychology of each per-son in particular, will you be able to achieve continuous performance improvement.

Take a look at a situation with one or more of your employees whose work could benefit from a PI effort. If you've implemented one before and have not achieved your desired results, review your actions in light of what you have just read. If you're about to start a PI initiative, save your-self a lot of trouble and aggravation and pay attention to the psychology of the performers from the beginning. You'll find that your improvement efforts proceed more easily and achieve greater results.

Finally, think back to the scenario that opened this chapter. The way we helped the PI consultant get the results that VCI wanted for its call center was to have her go in and personally interview all the people who were not performing up to the new standards. She asked them what it would take to get them to raise their performance levels and what they wanted as reinforcement. She then presented the resulting list to VCI and persuaded them to implement her solutions. Once they did this, performance improved and the company actually won an award for its high levels of customer service.

— *T W O* —

PERFORMANCE ENHANCEMENT

The Central Idea

I f you work with a personal trainer or work out at a health club, you know that a major focus of high-level fitness is to have a strong core. The fitness industry defines your core as your abdominal, hip, and back muscles, which basically support your entire body. That's why trainers have begun focusing on strengthening the core for people who want to attain overall fitness.

We began focusing on building a strong core more than twenty years ago, except that we were out to develop more fit business professionals. Our goal was and still is to link performance interventions and performance improvement to an enhancement process. We started focusing on strengths back then and we continue to focus on them throughout this book. Originally called performance enhancement programs, our projects were the precursor to this new approach to performance enhancement that we call Positive CORE.

Managers all want their performance improvement and enhancement programs to have flexibility, strength, and energy. We also call these adaptability, power, and commitment (emotional energy), which are the three things all performance interventions require to be successful. We talked about psychology in Chapter 1. Chapter 2 shows you how to consider the role emotions play in performance, as well as a variety of other people factors. Then we set out the foundation for the Positive CORE model, which is introduced with its components in Chapter 3.

THE EMOTIONAL SIDE OF PERFORMANCE IMPROVEMENT

In Chapter 1, we talked about the importance of putting the psychology of the people in a business ahead of the processes and models of performance improvement. Here we want to expand that focus so you become aware of people's needs, desires, and motivations. When you pay attention to the emotions and emotional states of performers, you stand a much better chance of realizing measurable improvements.

This section discusses how to overcome negative emotional states, manage stress effectively, and use the power of positive emotions to increase performance. Additionally, we describe both positive and negative emotions that you are likely to encounter in performers when you're working with them to create improvements.

EMOTIONAL STATES AND PERFORMANCE EXPECTATIONS

A performer's emotional state at the time of performance has a definite effect on that person's expectations of success. A positive emotional state will usually lead to positive expectations for success, while a negative state will do just the opposite. A poor performance does sometimes follow positive expectations, of course, and when this happens, the performer will respond based on previous experiences, becoming upset by the experience or accepting it as a lesson on how to improve for the next time. Be careful not to allow the people you're coaching to set unrealistic expectations for success—no amount of positive thinking will let a five-footer casually dunk a baseketball on a ten-foot rim. But despite the exceptions, the relationship between expectations, emotions, and performance outcomes is strong. What managers must realize is that people often fulfill their own prophecies, so the performance outcomes will reflect their expectations. These expectations will, in turn, affect four factors that are essential to effective performance enhancement: attention, focus, perception, and time on task.

Attention—Attention refers to how people tune in to the environmental stimuli that are essential to performing a task. There are two continua of attention—broad to narrow, and general to specific—which are determined by the performer, the task, and the environment. For example, a batter in a baseball game must pay narrow and specific attention to hit a pitched ball. A sales rep making a presentation to a CEO requires the same kind of attention. A guide on a safari has to have a broad and general type of attention, constantly aware of everything that is going on around the group. A computer repair tech also must pay broad and general attention at first to diagnose the problem, and then change to narrow and specific attention to complete the repairs.

Performers in every situation have to pay attention. How much attention they pay to their task definitely affects how well they perform. To improve performance, the manager needs to help people concentrate their attention on the task at hand and minimize distractions if distractions will be harmful.

Focus—Performers must be able to focus on what they are doing. If their minds are elsewhere because they are distracted or just not interested in the job, performance will suffer. Think of attendees at a business seminar.

So many things compete for their attention—the pressure of work left behind, for example, and their immediate personal reaction to the speaker or others in the group—that it is difficult for many of them to concentrate on one particular training task. So the trainer introduces an interactive task, which they do for a while with reasonable interest. Then they may be distracted again, and the initial task performance suffers.

Focus requires an almost meditative state of concentration. It is what people call mindfulness—but *mind fullness* might be better: keeping the mind *full* with the task at hand. When you ask performers to focus, you are asking them to stay tuned in to what they must do regardless of what is occurring around them. That's why football and basketball teams practice in stadiums and arenas with crowd noise piped in. The coaches want their players to remain focused on the task at hand despite the ongoing distractions. You can help people dramatically improve their performances if you just help them maintain the proper focus through emotional control.

Perception—The level of emotional control will affect a performer's perception of the situation. People who are very upset or angry tend to perceive things differently than those who are relaxed. And people who are in a state of optimal arousal (emotional control) perceive events differently than everyone else. In fact, when you are in a state of optimal emotional arousal, you can experience what is commonly called flow, which we mentioned before. Being in flow means your attention is properly focused, the task is challenging, and your emotions are in an optimal arousal state, so the performance can just happen with minimal or no conscious intervention. In other words, you are not thinking about what you are doing; you are just doing it.

When performers are in flow, their perceptions become very acute and their emotions reach a state of euphoria. Time and motion seem to slow down, movement and thought become effortless, and positive emotions flood the mind-body system. If you can help people achieve this state of flow more often, not only will their perceptions improve, but their overall performances and productivity will greatly improve. One of the ways to do this is to create a task that is challenging and meaningful and that, when properly completed, will enhance the performer's self-esteem.

Time on task—The last area that the emotional state of the performer affects is the time on task. Performers who are in a positive emotional state (flow state) can perform indefinitely. Since "time stands still," they just keep on going. However, when performers are in a negative emotional state, they will do anything to get away from the task. Minutes drag on like hours, and every activity related to completing the task is drudgery. The negative emotional state begins to cycle on itself and cause a continuing decrease in performance.

Improving performance in this situation requires a change in the job, the environment, the reward, the recognition system for performing the job, or the praise system (which is another way of saying you should tell people when they're doing a good job). It's not that we are trying to increase the time on task so that people stay on the job indefinitely. The real goal is to determine the time needed to complete the task effectively and make sure that performers are in the proper emotional state to remain at the job and perform it well for the time required.

STRESS AND PERFORMANCE

Everyone is familiar with the idea of stress and the way it affects human life. The paradox is that there is no such thing as stress. Stress is only a perceptual manifestation of emotional and physical reactions to stimuli based on past experiences. True, people have physiological reactions to stress that can be tested in laboratories as well as displayed as certain behaviors. But the reality is that the perception of and response to situations determines whether they are truly stressful.

The major stresses of life and the day-to-day hassles and minor upsets affect performance equally. You can go through the motions of performing on the job or playing a sport, but if your *emotions* are messed up, your performance will suffer. We see this happen all the time in sports, and it's a constant factor in the workplace, too.

People who feel excessive stress do not perform well. To generate a significant performance improvement, help people identify their personal and work-related sources of stress, how they react to them, and what they can do to manage their stress levels. Without going into a treatise on stress management, let us suggest that you work on the following as you try to improve people's performance.

Get them to acknowledge that stress is a perceptual phenomenon and that different people will respond to stressful stimuli differently. Although this seems like so much common sense, you would be surprised how many stressed-out people cannot understand why the rest of the world isn't stressed out too. So, the first step in alleviating debilitating stress is to get performers to admit that they are responding to certain situations negatively. Then you can help them develop the characteristics of psychological hardiness, resilience, and self-control.

Psychological hardiness is the ability of a performer to resist life stressors and avoid succumbing to stress-related illnesses. People who possess psychological hardiness perform under stress with more commitment, and they feel a sense of challenge (consider the flow state) and control (self-efficacy). You can readily see how this concept relates to both athletes and workers, since both possess a strong commitment to their work, their goals, and their relationships. Rather than being alienated or withdrawing under stress, hardy people remain actively engaged in whatever they are doing, stay connected to the people around them, and continue to believe that their efforts will make a difference. In the face of ongoing performance-related stress, these people can find the will and the motivation to continually improve their performance while bouncing back from adversity.

The ability to handle adversity, also known as *resilience,* is a primary factor in overcoming stress and other obstacles. Resilient performers know that what matters is not how many times you get knocked down but how many times you get back up. They are aware that performance mastery includes many peaks and valleys, as well as a significant number of plateaus. People who are not resilient tend to give up when they find themselves at a plateau. Witness sales professionals who get into a slump (performance decrease or plateau) and cannot seem to find a way out. Some of them keep doing the same thing over and over again, expecting different results (a definition of insanity), while others bemoan their fate and become paralyzed. Still others become superstitious and try a number of different remedies that worked in the past in hopes that they will work now. Unfortunately, the problem is really twofold. First, people sometimes take the slump as a hit to their self-esteem. This automatically lowers performance and makes any improvement difficult. Second, non-resilient performers don't realize that plateaus are a natural part of learning and performance. They occur as your mind and body are adjusting to their new skill sets. Pretty soon, if you just accept the plateau and continue to be resilient and resourceful, you will find an upward spike in performance.

The third element to performing under stress (pressure) is *self-control.* This is the performer's ability to have an effect on the job, the environment, or other people. It also relates to the concept of emotional intelligence, wherein people need to be able to control their emotions in stress-filled situations in order to perform well.

When people are under stress, they need to know what they are capable of, how their performance will affect the task or environment, and what they must do to achieve the desired results. Since uncertainty and unpredictability are major sources of behavioral and performance-related stress, people want to know what is expected of them, how the task should be played out, and what consequences will occur once they complete the performance. When you provide these elements to a performer and combine them with typical approaches to stress management, such as relaxation and visualization, you set the stage for significant performance improvement. The goal is to use hardiness, resilience, and self-control to transform stress, which everyone experiences, into positive energy that increases current performance, provides a foundation for improvement in future performances, and makes work flow.

NEGATIVE EMOTIONS THAT HINDER PERFORMANCE

Many negative emotions and mental states can affect performance, but we've found that these ten are the primary culprits:

- **Fear:** An emotion that occurs when the performer does not have control over the stimulus situation and also may not know the outcome of certain behaviors. In most cases, fear can be thought of as an acronym—FEAR, standing for "false expectations appearing real."

- **Anxiety:** The tension produced by a situation that involves uncertainty, unpredictability, a perceived lack of control, or a threat to a person's self-esteem.

- **Anger (which leads to aggression):** A natural emotion most often manifested in negative ways, through either physical or verbal abuse. Sometimes anger is also displayed as passive-aggressive behavior.

- **Frustration:** An emotion generated when the performer cannot control the outcome of the performance, either because the situational environment is limiting or the required skill set is lacking.

- **Sadness:** A common reaction to the inability to perform well or achieve a goal. It can lead to feelings of despair.

- **Depression:** A response to intense, long-lasting sadness. In a performance situation, it is usually the result of continued failure.

- **Detachment:** A sense of alienation from others. When performers feel they don't belong, they detach from the performance situation as well as from the people around them.

- **Confusion:** A mental state that leads to inability to make decisions, make choices, or complete a task. It results from too much stress, anxiety, fear, or any of the negative emotions.

- **Shame:** A reaction to the embarrassment of not completing a task or doing well at an assignment. It usually relates to how performers feel others will perceive them.

- **Distraction:** An inability to maintain concentration and focus on the task at hand. People also get distracted when too many instructions on how to perform a task are being thrown at them or there is too much going on in their environment.

All of these negative emotions or mental states are harmful to performance and attempts at improvement. They impede learning, adversely affect performance, and ultimately perpetuate a negative cycle. Once a negative emotion is repeatedly linked (anchored) to a poor performance or an inability to improve, it tends to strengthen that negative relationship. This then leads to other negative emotions, and feelings of helplessness or unworthiness start to creep over the performer. Next, self-esteem is lowered and performance continues to decrease. Ultimately, the performer just cannot seem to learn how to improve the performance.

At this point, all the technical and technological interventions in the world will not help. It's as if the person has given up on improving performance. It is up to the HPT specialist to create an environment in which the performer experiences a series of successful events and positive emotions flourish. Only when that is done is it reasonable to consider working on improving performance.

POSITIVE EMOTIONS THAT HELP PERFORMANCE

A host of positive emotions will help improve performance. Unfortunately, people seem to be able to name more negative emotions than positive ones. They have to look a little harder and a little deeper to find the positive emotions that come into play during a good performance. This task can become easier if you just ask people who are experiencing flow what else they are feeling.

Here are ten positive emotions or mental states that can help anyone engaged in an actual performance or trying to create a performance improvement situation:

- **Joy, happiness, elation:** Three names for one of the most natural emotions—and one that is not experienced often enough during any type of performance. If performing can be fun, happiness naturally follows because of the intrinsic satisfaction derived from the performance.

- **Achievement motivation:** A measurable construct of risk-taking behavior that tells us how much risk a person is willing to take in order to achieve a goal.

- **Approach motivation:** The positive side of a motivation continuum between approach and avoidance. People with this outlook will actively seek outcomes they desire instead of working to avoid those they fear.

- **Appreciation:** The number one need of all people. We show appreciation in many ways, and the more ways and times we show it to performers, the better they will perform.

- **Relaxation:** A mental and physical state that is highly effective at reducing stress, increasing visualization abilities, and improving performance in a variety of endeavors.

- **Confidence:** The feeling people have when they truly believe in themselves and their ability to achieve goals. Self-confidence can elevate performance to levels much higher than any training program or other performance intervention.

- **Engagement:** A state of absorption in a performance, wherein performers are totally involved with what they are doing. It is part of the flow concept.

- **Faith:** Performers who believe in themselves and their capabilities can also believe in improvement interventions—at which point, success is inevitable.

- **Pride:** The feeling that accompanies accomplishment. Being proud of something done well helps performers grow and increases their motivation to do well.

- **Enthusiasm:** A positive feeling toward a task and its accomplishment that also leads to peak performances, happiness, and a great deal of self-esteem.

Focus on arousing these positive emotions and mental states in the performers you are trying to influence and you will generate significant improvements. But remember one thing about emotions and motivation: you can never really create emotions in someone else, nor can you motivate someone else. The only thing a PI specialist can do is create the conditions that will enable people to motivate themselves, to feel good about themselves, and to expect to succeed. This expectancy of success will lead to greater and greater confidence in future performances, along with an increased desire to keep improving. As long as you provide the right conditions, performance improvement will occur. Sometimes this improvement will be incremental, and other times it will be a quantum leap. In any case, it will occur as long as the performer is in a positive emotional state.

In summary, you want to increase some emotions and mental states and decrease others. The positive ones will improve performance, while the negative ones will hinder performance. When you increase the positive emotional aspects related to a performance, you increase the psychological and physical energy levels of performers, their expectancy of success, their levels of self-esteem, their motivation to do whatever it takes to get better (that is, their commitment), and their ability to learn and perform new tasks.

One other point we want to make here involves the concept of *emotional security,* the state that allows performers to know that they can make mistakes and learn from them. It requires that performers not be punished when they don't exhibit a peak performance every time. And it enables performers to "fail forward." Everyone makes mistakes in life. Most of them are not earth shattering or mind blowing, yet bosses, colleagues, and parents often overreact. It's better to consider the situation in which the mistake was made, the emotional state of the performer, and the outcome that occurred. Then you can make a constructive determination about how to handle the person and the situation.

The reactions any individual's performance elicits have a tremendous effect on whether that person will perform again. Think of an infant learning to walk. Parents applaud each step, voicing encouragement and even providing "job aids" (things the infant can hold on to, role models, and mechanical devices such as walkers) to help improve the performance. Despite hundreds of failures, children still continue to pick themselves up "one more time than they fall down," and eventually they improve enough to walk.

Performers need the same treatment at any age. If you coach youth sports, you can take the same type of motivation and encouragement that you use with the kids on your team and apply it in the workplace with adults. If you teach Sunday school or religious classes, you can use the same type of encouragement. Take care of your workers' emotions the same way you take care of your children's or players' emotions. Your goal in every situation is to help the performer achieve a highly positive emotional state—and continued success.

OTHER PEOPLE FACTORS IN PERFORMANCE IMPROVEMENT

Wherever we have gone for the past twenty years, whether consulting and training for corporations or speaking before groups and professional organizations, we have heard the same question: "How do I improve my performance and then sustain that improvement?" It is a simple question, really. And the answer is actually very simple too: spend less time on external issues—task analysis, work design, ergonomics, job aids, organizational restructuring, team building, and so on—and more time focusing directly on people. When you focus your attention on the people factors in performance improvement, you get the results you are looking for, and then some.

Several years ago, a client (we will call her Barbara) came to us for help. She was in her late twenties, in what she called a "dead-end job," going nowhere in her personal or professional life, and just basically depressed. Traditional employee assistance programs, job counseling, and job retraining had not helped her improve her performance. She told us she was going to lose her job even though she understood its requirements very well. In talking with Barbara, we noticed that she had no purpose and no goals to which she could commit her energies. She also lacked three important ingredients that would make her a successful performer: a good self-image, a high level of self-esteem, and a positive attitude toward the world. Instead, she had a poor self-image coupled with low self-esteem, and her attitude toward everything was negative.

No wonder nothing her employer tried worked. The measures were all external to Barbara, and the real problem was internal. Her employer neglected the people side of Barbara's performance improvement efforts.

We worked with Barbara for three months. Our efforts included personal coaching and personal mastery skills training. In that time, Barbara identified a personal purpose for her life, wrote down her goals, improved her self-image, gained a positive attitude, became intrinsically motivated, and began to perform better at work. Her boss could not believe the change in her. Where she was once being counseled that her job was in jeopardy, she was now being applauded for her superior performance. Her personal and professional lives turned around dramatically.

Afterword: One month after we completed our work together, Barbara left that job and got a new one at twice the salary. Every time we spoke, she thanked us for "making" her successful. The truth is, we had nothing to do with it, or at least very little. We may have given her the keys to success, but she had to open the doors and walk through.

We have found the following people factors, which managers must pay attention to for themselves as well as for their performers, to be major keys to positive performance improvement:

- Positive attitude
- High self-esteem and positive self-image
- Communication skills
- Lifelong learning
- Love
- Health and well-being
- Motivation
- Goal setting
- Relaxation
- Visualization
- Personal value system

POSITIVE ATTITUDE

You must have a positive attitude toward yourself first, and then toward everything you do and everyone you meet. Say positive things to yourself every day (affirmations), and talk to yourself in a positive manner (positive self-talk). You have to know that you are responsible for all the outcomes of your behavior (attributions). And you have to believe in the general good of all people.

Many authors, consultants, and speakers talk about how this approach and attitude will lead to many positive things happening for you. It sets in motion "cosmic forces" that will bring good things into your life. Now, you do not have to believe them or us, but just think back to the times when what felt like happy coincidence or good luck came into your life. Were you thinking about certain things and wanting them to happen? And then they happened! Was it just coincidence and synchronicity, or did you really have something to do with it? Was it your attitude that led to the new achievements?

We know it was you, and so do you. Think positively, and your performance will definitely improve. Help your people to do the same. This positive attitude will also open many other doors to success.

HIGH SELF-ESTEEM AND POSITIVE SELF-IMAGE

What you think of yourself speaks volumes about who you are and how people respond to you. Having high self-esteem establishes a positive achievement cycle in your life. Your positive self-image attracts other people to you. These people want to be around you, and, either consciously or unconsciously, they want to help you succeed. Because of all this, your performance improves.

You build a high level of self-esteem through your positive attitude and by having confidence in yourself as a person. Believe that you can do anything you set your mind to do. You can achieve any level of performance that you make up your mind to achieve, as long as it is realistic according to your physiological and psychological makeup. Measure your self-worth according to your own standards.

As a manager, you can build your own self-esteem while you are building the self-esteem of your employees. Do things that feel good and right for you and that generate the same feelings and responses in other people. If you want other people to compliment you, compliment them first. If you want other people to make you feel good, which will build your self-esteem, do something to make other people feel good first. You can always be successful at building your own self-esteem if you help others build theirs first. And you can always improve your performance by helping other people improve theirs.

Here is a somewhat ethereal concept that we know has an effect on the people side of performance improvement: When you help other people do better, this raises their self-esteem and improves their attitude. Then the world and the universe conspire to help *you* improve and get what *you* want. This raises your self-esteem and keeps your positive attitude going. When people feel good about themselves and others around them, performance increases. It becomes a virtuous cycle.

COMMUNICATION SKILLS

Positive performers are successful people who are also great communicators. They are able to convince, influence, and persuade others, and to communicate their ideas, dreams, and goals to other people as well, enlisting their aid to achieve those goals. Also, these people are excellent listeners. In fact, if you ever want to be remembered as a great conversationalist, just listen.

Effective communication is only effective based on the response you get. If you do not get the other person to grasp what you're talking about, respond the way you intended, or understand what you expect regarding the performance, then you have not been effective as a communicator. This is one of the main causes for people not accomplishing what they set out to do. They just do not understand the task at hand, what is expected of them, or how they should go about performing.

Communication is also the key to success in all interpersonal relationships, and it is a foundational element of the people side of positive performance improvement. How do you get to be an effective communicator so that you can help people improve their performance? You learn about others. Learn their speaking style, the words they use, and the outcomes they are looking for when they communicate. Then feed this back to them by flexing your style and you will see a magnificent change occur as you develop rapport. It gets to the point where you think you know what other people are going to say before they say it—but stops short of the point where you act on that belief rather than on what actually gets said.

Another clue to using this key to successful performance improvement effectively is to remember how you feel when someone shuts the door on you. You try to get them to communicate (give you feedback) but nothing seems to work. You are out there all alone, feeling lost and sometimes helpless. Make sure you communicate effectively, especially when you are providing feedback, and everyone's performance will improve.

LIFELONG LEARNING

Successful people are constantly learning. They read, go to seminars, watch specific programs on television, listen to tapes, and do everything possible to learn whatever they can about their area of endeavor. Not only that, they enjoy being mentors and coaches to other people who are motivated to learn for life. Successful organizations promote this behavior among their staff members. So, regardless of where you stopped your formal education, now is the time to start learning again. The more you learn, the more you will improve.

LOVE

Volumes have been written on the subject of love. Just look at how many of these books line the shelves at bookstores. All we want to say is that you have to love yourself before you can love others. The more love you give, the more you will get back in return. At work, consider showing you care about other people. We are not talking about romantic love here; just good old-fashioned caring, concern, and understanding. This concept has tremendous application in the workplace. When people know you care about them, they will do whatever they can to please you and make you happy. They will evidence this by being extra nice to you, upgrading their skills, and improving their performances. For a small effort on your part, you can get a tremendous return on your investment. And remember, you can never give more love to someone else than you are capable of giving yourself or receiving from someone else.

HEALTH AND WELL-BEING

Take care of yourself. Eat right, think right, get enough exercise. When you look and feel good, the world seems to be a better place. People who are healthy and well simply perform better. They have more energy and more stamina, and they can deal more effectively with stress.

Most PI issues or problems have a stress component related to them. People under too much stress—or too little for that matter—do not perform as well as they should. In fact, performance suffers significantly in most cases. So one key in the relationship between health and top performance is to determine your optimal stress or arousal level for a particular performance. Also, when you are well, you can manage your stress better, which enables you to perform at a higher level.

It may be as simple as relaxing a little bit more instead of trying so hard. Or you may have to review what is causing your stress and eliminate some of the sources from your life. In any case, how you feel at any given time, the mood you are in, and your overall thought patterns will affect your performance. To be a top performer, be well, do well, and live well.

MOTIVATION

Motivation is another factor that is so important that stacks of books have been written about it. The door to successful performance improvement opens wide for you when you are intrinsically motivated. That means your desires and your satisfaction with performance come from within, not from some external source of rewards.

You also need to determine your level of achievement motivation. What is it you truly want to achieve, and how much are you willing to risk getting it? Do you want to be involved in tasks that are so simple anyone can achieve them, or do you want to be involved with accomplishing something with a moderate to high degree of difficulty? Your answers to these questions will identify your achievement motivation related to your performances.

Another aspect of motivation involves its direction. Do you move toward a goal or away from it? Do you have a fear of success or a fear of failure? Are you willing to put more effort into achieving pleasure, or will avoiding some sort of pain motivate you to action? These are real factors in determining how well you use this key to performance success, so you must know what causes you to act, how you interpret your actions, and what you plan to do about similar situations the next time.

Here is one more thing that makes this performance factor work effectively. You must develop your own reward systems. When you determine the rewards for your performances, you stay intrinsically motivated. If you establish many external rewards, or let your company establish the rewards for you without your involvement, you will find your motivation and your associated performance levels decreasing over time. So make sure you know exactly what you want when you succeed and how you will reinforce and reward yourself.

GOAL SETTING

Goal setting is closely aligned with motivation. Most people never set goals. Of those who do, less than 5 percent actually write their goals down. It is this small percentage of people who have a purpose in life to which they can be committed.

You must write down your goals for performance improvement and be very specific about the outcomes you are trying to achieve. What will goal attainment or success look, sound, and feel like? What are the measurements that will let you know your performance has improved? How will you know you have gotten the exact outcome you wanted? And what results or changes in behavior will be evident so that you will know your goal has been reached?

Make all your goal statements personal, measurable, and set within a reasonable time frame, and make sure they are outcome oriented rather than action oriented. Statements about what you are going to do tend to leave out what you are going to accomplish, so they are not enough to guarantee goal attainment and success. You need to have outcome-oriented criteria for success so that you will know exactly when you've achieved your goal.

RELAXATION

Relaxation is a performance factor that permeates all the others. It helps you visualize your way to successful PI, manage stress, engage in positive self-talk, build and rebuild your self-image, and train your mind and body for peak performance. You must engage in some form of relaxation every day.

You can relax by breathing deeply, alternately tensing and relaxing your muscles, picturing yourself in a relaxing and stress-free environment, engaging in a hobby, or exercising. Whatever you do, realize that tension, stress, and relaxation cannot coexist. Usually, when people are trying to improve their performance, they end up trying too hard. The result is increased stress, pressure, or anxiety and a less-than-stellar performance. If you just relax and let things happen (let them flow), you will find that your performance will keep improving.

The other benefit to relaxation is that all, and we do mean all, peak performances come when your mind and body are in a state of relaxed alertness. You are ready to perform at your peak and you are willing to let your mind and body work together without conscious intervention. This is the state of flow, in which all your body and brain systems work together perfectly. It is that desired state that everyone tries to attain. When you are in a state of flow, you do not have to try so hard to achieve. In fact, you feel like you are not even trying at all. Successful performances just happen. So relax, enter a state of flow, and achieve and improve.

Managers should always work to create the conditions that allow employees to experience a state of relaxed alertness so they can become top performers. Some employees work well under pressure, while others fold under pressure. It is the manager's job to identify the people who thrive in the pressure cooker and give it to them in reasonable doses while simultaneously keeping the others out of harm's way.

VISUALIZATION

Visualization is the process of imagining yourself improving and being successful. Since real memories and imagined events feel the same, when you picture yourself improving and being successful, at some level your mind will accept that picture as fact. Then it will do everything in its power to make that image a reality.

Visualization is a skill that can be developed and nurtured. It can be used to erase bad past performances and to develop future positive behaviors. Witness the performance breakthroughs that have been achieved by skilled practitioners of neurolinguistic programming (NLP). NLP is a branch of psychology and human performance that involves language (linguistic) to program the nervous system (neuro). NLP focuses on how you code experiences (performances) in your mind and memory. Much of what makes NLP so effective and successful is its use of visualization as a behavior change medium.

Also, when you combine visualization with relaxation and goal setting, you establish a pattern that leads to continuous self-improvement, successful performance improvement, and achievement.

PERSONAL VALUE SYSTEM

This may be the most important key to performance improvement and your ultimate success. Without a value system, you will not be able to make decisions, define your true purpose in life, and carry out the behaviors necessary to achieve your goals.

Values are the foundation for all you do. Your decisions and behavioral choices are based on your value system. You choose the people you associate with and relate to based on your values. When your behaviors are incongruent with your values, you feel tremendous discomfort. You no longer function optimally, either psychologically or physically. The result is poor performance, a deteriorating relationship, or a negative attitude toward yourself. Identify your values, clarify them, and understand how they relate to your performance. Then you will see tremendous performance improvements as your value system guides your achievement behaviors.

OUR CHALLENGE TO YOU

You have just been introduced to eleven key people factors of performance improvement. These eleven factors are the true foundation of *human* performance technology. Employers, companies, and individuals that begin to focus on the performers first and the characteristics that make each one unique will realize significant performance improvements on a regular basis.

You must also consider the role emotions play in PI efforts. The last word on dealing with the emotional side of performance improvement is simple. You simply cannot ignore the effect that *affect*—emotional tone— has on performance. Stimulate your performers, support their efforts, help them motivate themselves, and you will see performance improvements that initially looked impossible. What people will achieve when they have emotional security, support for their self-esteem, and a challenging task to perform will go beyond the results that the typical technical and technological tools yield. People will definitely achieve above and beyond your expectations. That's because their emotions are involved, they are committed to getting better, and they know they will continue to feel good about themselves after repeated successes.

We challenge you to become enough of an amateur psychologist to help your people improve. Go back and review the concepts related to the psychology of performers, what makes them tick, goal setting, the mental state of performers, and how their emotions affect their performance. You must help performers train their own brains to maximize their gain—and yours.

— *THREE* —

POSITIVE CORE MODEL

Your Performance Improvement Guarantee

Richard writes about an event that occurred over forty years ago that remains indelibly imprinted on his memory. Looking back, he can see that it started him on his philosophy about a positive approach to performance improvement.

It was the worst day of my life. Or so it seemed at the time. We were fin-ishing a spelling test in second grade. The last word on the test was friend. *I spelled it correctly, then had my doubts, tried to erase it, tried to cover up the erasure, then firmly committed to changing it to "freind." This must be correct, I thought. After all, I always get 100 percent on my spelling tests. I never missed a word since I started school, so this had to be right.*

A few days later, I got my test back. I got a 95 percent. I got friend *wrong. You can be sure that now, over four decades later, I'll never forget how to spell it. And why is it so indelibly etched in my memory? Partly it is because I got it wrong on that test. But I believe the most traumatic part of the experience was when I asked the teacher about the word. My teacher was unbelievable, and not in a good way. She couldn't believe that her high-performing student got a word wrong on the test.*

So what do you think she focused on? Do you think she congratulated me on the 95 or do you think she grilled me on why I got the word wrong?

You guessed it. My teacher was only focused on the wrong answer. Forget the fact that I scored 100 percent on every other spelling test and that I was an overall A student. And forget the fact that this second grader was visibly upset with missing the word. My teacher only wanted to drill down into why I got the word wrong.

And that's what happens in schools and businesses around the world today. People focus on what went wrong, what was done wrong, where the mistakes were made, why the mistakes were made, and what must be done to improve things. Unfortunately, they rarely focus on what was done right and how it was done right.

Now shift gears to the business arena and think about the annual performance evaluation. It is a ritual most managers and employees despise, for a variety of reasons. Most evaluation or appraisal meetings involve the manager and the employee sitting down to review the employee's performance. The manager touches briefly—if at all—on the accomplishments of the past year and then spends most of the time going over what went wrong. The manager feels uncomfortable and the employee is not happy either. And then, if the review is negative and there is no salary increase (which the employee expects to receive regardless of the review), all hell can break loose.

That's typical of performance evaluations. Even though everyone knows that people respond better to positive reinforcement or at least acknowledgment of what they have accomplished, most managers do not say a thing when all is well. People who work in such an environment soon come to believe that if they're not hearing anything negative, things must be all right. Since it feels like they always hear about problems, they naturally assume that silence means success.

Nobody likes to live or perform in a vacuum. People want, even crave, feedback—especially positive feedback, but criticism is also useful. And someone who hears from the boss only when things go wrong will live in fear or anxiety for an extended period if an error occurs shortly after the annual performance review. Will it make a difference next year? This fear or anxiety is compounded if the boss does not say anything at the time even though the normal response would be to point out the wrongdoing to the employee. Now the employee will spend the ensuing months until the next review wondering whether the boss noticed what happened. This same problem exists in the field of performance improvement.

NEGATIVE APPROACHES TO PERFORMANCE IMPROVEMENT

Most current approaches to performance improvement focus on the negative. They look for gaps, problems, and things that are wrong. The systems, models, and processes are all set up to help internal and external performance improvement consultants (and managers who are so designated by default) find something wrong that can and must be corrected. It is as if something must be wrong so someone's existence can be justified.

It's like anything else in life: you will always find what you are looking for as long as you stay focused on it. For example, if you want to catch someone doing something right, you can always find an action, behavior, or statement to acknowledge and praise. Conversely, if you want to find someone doing something wrong, as often happens when a company wants to document an employee out of a job, you can always find an action, behavior, or statement that is wrong or somehow not up to par.

As the old saying goes, if all you have is a hammer, then everything looks like a nail. In this case, if you're looking to implement a performance improvement solution, you will definitely find a problem. In fact, PI consultants have often been called solution providers in search of a problem.

But it's not their fault. The models they currently use promote this negative approach.

CURRENT PI MODELS

Look at some of the models in use today. Take the *ADDIE model* (analysis, design, development, implementation, evaluation), which is really an instructional systems design model that has been carried over to performance improvement. The ADDIE model has the consultant analyzing what is wrong in a curriculum, performance, or learning situation, or looking for what is missing in the current educational offering. The rest of the model describes a process to be followed that plugs the gap when a new learning program has been created.

Or consider *front-end analysis,* which is an enhanced version of the type of needs analysis most people will conduct. In any case, this type of analysis specifies finding a gap, problem, or weakness. The next step is to determine or develop potential solutions and then to select one solution to implement, in the hope that the implementation will close the gap, solve the problem, or overcome the weakness. This is a lofty goal for everyone to strive for. Yet where and when does the performer get positively reinforced for any accomplishments or achievements if all we are focusing on are the gaps between what is and what we'd like it to be?

One of the more famous models for PI is *Gilbert's behavioral engineering model,* which gives you six categories to examine for performance problems. These categories include three "issues" that are specific to the performer and three that are specific to the organization or environment. Any one of these six issues can negatively affect the outcome of a performance, just as any one can be used as an intervention. Gilbert's model has been adapted, updated, and even expanded in the ways it has been used in the PI field. There is no denying that the model works, but again, it is used to specify or identify a gap or a problem. It leaves out several issues that are important to successful performance, such as the performer's motivation, the meaning and relevance of the action to the performer, and a way to expand or enhance current positive performance outcomes (discussed in Chapter 2).

With all these models looking for problems—and usually finding them (managers and PI consultants do have to justify their existence)—it's no wonder that the field is full of of solution providers in search of a problem.

Before we move on, we want to acknowledge two models that serve a dual purpose. Carl Binder has adapted the *behavioral engineering model* in an attempt to make it simpler and more applicable for clients and practitioners. His approach still seeks to find performance gaps, yet his work on developing *fluency* provides an approach to achieving high levels of performance.

The other model is Roger Kaufman's *organizational elements model* (OEM). Kaufman proposes five levels of this model, ranging from inputs and processes to micro-, macro-, and megaresults. While this model can also identify gaps in performance for both individuals and organizations, Kaufman's focus on the *mega* (the ideal vision or highest achievable performance goal) gives users a way to take an already positive or excellent performance and strive to make it even better.

MORE PROBLEMS WITH THE PROBLEM APPROACH

Today's approaches pose two more major difficulties that must be overcome. The first is selling the performance improvement concept to CEOs, whether as an internal provider or an external consultant. CEOs just don't see the value of PI, and this is probably because the experts come in with a problem without having a solution. Or someone in the organization identifies what looks like a problem and announces that training or something else that will cost a lot of money is the solution. These are obstacles that must be overcome if you want to get the ear of the CEO.

The second issue is that even given the green light, a performance improvement project is difficult to implement. Funds and resources tend to be scarce, time pressure is high, not enough expert implementers can be found, and other factors intervene. In addition, the people the PI experts maintain they are helping to improve buy in at the most minimal levels, and the experts are left wondering why. Remember, no one likes to be constantly reminded that they have to improve.

Convincing C-level Executives—Let's look first at the issue of communicating PI-speak to CEOs. The PI field uses terms like *systems, systemic, systems analysis* (sometimes confused with computers), *needs assessment, needs analysis, interventions,* and *levels of effect.* These terms are usually understandable by CEOs and other decision makers when we make a compelling case for them. However, the problem is that these terms are techno-speak for the PI literati. They are not the terms or language a CEO would use. A CEO talks in terms of *productivity, performance,* and *profitability* and wants to know about *return on investment (ROI), total cost of ownership, time to benefit,* and things related to these calculations. Management buy-in requires using a shared language that both sides understand.

The waters get even murkier if you also have to convince a CFO, who is primarily focused on the dollars and cents, of the value of your work. Table 1 gives you an idea of the areas you have to cover when you communicate the value of PI to a CEO, CFO, or any other C-level executive, for that matter. Keep in mind also that maybe these people are tired of hearing what is wrong and what has to be improved and are looking to hear what is right and can be made even better.

Implementing Your PI Project—Let's take a positive approach to the C-level issue. You have convinced the C-level executive to fund your performance improvement effort. Now it is up to you to engage the players, find the resources, make sure the tools are available, and ensure that the implementation takes place so that the expected results are achieved. You see, simply getting the blessing of the C-level executive does not guarantee a smooth implementation of your procedures or selected intervention. You still have a rough road ahead, especially because you are going

TABLE 1: CONVINCING C-LEVEL EXECUTIVES ABOUT PI

CEO
- Wants PI to provide better information and improved business processes
- Sees technology (HPT or computer) as secondary to results
- Prefers to adopt solutions that are 80 percent usable as is and 20 percent customizable instead of building from scratch
- Wants strategic relationships with vendors to leapfrog the competition if the improvement cannot be managed in-house
- Regards investment costs as secondary to ROI and total cost of ownership
- Needs to believe that PI must be an agent of change and integrated into the corporate culture
- Needs to understand how PI creates a competitive advantage and increases revenue

CFO
- Wants a sound business reason for investment
- Looks for consistency of PI with the longer-range corporate strategy
- Requires a sound execution plan
- Wants to know when to do PI and with which technology or approach
- Cares about expected return on investment
- Compares the cost of building with the cost of buying (internal versus external practitioners)
- Looks for measurable deliverables in individual performance and financials

BENEFITS
- Expects internal cost reductions from new process efficiencies
- Looks for clear advantages for high-level performance
- Wants ease of use of the new performance system
- Expects increased performer involvement
- Wants to hear about new opportunities resulting from high-performing people
- Needs metrics that are relevant to corporate performance
- Needs upper management support to integrate a PI approach into the company
- Can train staff on PI and associated languages and technologies
- Looks for a phased-in approach of the new performance culture
- Expects ongoing use of PI to increase performance

to tell your employees that they have been performing below expectations and now you have the solution to their problem.

Be prepared. You will meet resistance. This resistance may seem hard to understand, but the view from the psychological terrace makes it very clear. People resist this type of behavior change because they are being told their current behaviors are not good enough. Once again, they are told about all the things they are doing wrong without being told what they are doing right. Or they are told they did something right and the rest wrong, and here is how they should change or improve what is wrong.

Put yourself in your employees' shoes, or those of any performer, for that matter. How would you or do you feel about doing something new or different after your ego has taken a hit? Are you going to run right out there and jump into the improvement activity with both feet, or are you going to hang back a little bit and either see what happens or hope this focus on so-called improvement goes away? Take some time to think about your answer. We are sure that your employees will find the same reasons you do for avoiding a performance improvement intervention when it is presented this way.

So, what can you do about it? Think back to the past and take a lesson from helping a child learn to walk. Remember all that positive reinforcement? As a baby tries to get up and walk and promptly falls down, no one yells about messing up. We don't berate the child for not being able to walk. No, we applaud and positively reinforce each attempted step. The baby becomes engaged in mastering the task—proceeding much faster because of the positive reinforcement—and eventually does learn to walk.

Any performance improvement effort requires a similarly positive approach. What works is to acknowledge that performance must be improved while at the same time presenting the case in a positive light. If you try that, just maybe, people will listen to you, embrace your ideas, and implement your suggestions to strengthen themselves and their organizations.

A POSITIVE APPROACH TO PI

As we said before, the performance improvement field currently has a deficiency mind-set. A multitude of models and theories point out how to find out what is wrong with an organization or performer. These models and theories focus on a specific area of performance (individual, systems, or subsystems) and identify what is wrong with performance in that area. The idea is to determine whether the deficiency is due to the system, the environment, the incentives provided by the organization, the lack of a societal vision, the lack of resources, the lack of a good performer-task fit, the lack of mastery levels of skill, the lack of . . .

As you can see, it's an industry of *lack.* Or is it an industry of *missing links,* since it looks for what is missing between the current state and the desired state of performance, also known as gaps, and then attempts to create "something" to link the two states so that future performances approximate the desired goal? The approaches that have been followed for so many years deserve a long, hard look because they have not gotten buy-in or the results that knowledgeable and concerned professionals— with which the HPT field is well supplied—would normally expect.

POSITIVE PSYCHOLOGY

Martin Seligman, of learned helplessness fame, describes a similar approach in psychology. He says that the entire field of psychology has been built on a foundation of pathology. Every year, the diagnostic manual grows in size as it describes what is wrong with people, their minds, and their behaviors.

To overcome this deficiency approach, Seligman and several colleagues proposed an approach they call "positive psychology." This approach to psychology and performance has caught on so rapidly that there are now conferences on the topic, books of 500+ pages describing the effects of positive psychology in multiple areas of life, and a host of research projects that have yielded results supporting this approach over the deficiency approach. Seligman and his colleagues have created many models and strategy checklists to move the positive psychology field forward. One such list, shown in Table 2, includes twelve strategies or skills that build personal strength, values, and character.

These twelve strategies form one of the foundations for positive psychology, and those of us in the field of HPT would do well to consider them as integral to our own success. Like other aspects of positive psychology, they focus on the individual performer and what that individual brings to the situation. The combination of positive psychology and the strengths psychology approach (the Gallup model) makes great sense for efforts to improve overall performance. It lends tremendous credence to what we lovingly call "the messy middle": that space where models and analytics may not work but that definitely exists and has an effect on performance. That is why we urge HPT practitioners to focus on both the messy middle and the positive approach to what is right instead of a negative approach to what is wrong.

Positive psychology looks for what is good in an individual or an organization, what strengths can be duplicated and emulated, what the superpositive results will be when new types of interventions are implemented. It sets aside the search for pathology and looks for what is right with people. Practitioners need to learn the psychological makeup and techniques that help people not only survive but thrive. A great deal of recent research by the Gallup group on discovering and enhancing people's strengths fits in with this premise.

Tiger Woods presents a great example of playing to your strengths. Even though he is the best golfer in the world, he still has aspects of his game that he must work on. Yet instead of focusing on his weaknesses, he works to enhance his strengths. He practices constantly to become even stronger at what he does best. He works on driving the ball for distance with greater accuracy instead of just shortening his drives to achieve greater accuracy. This also keeps him out of the sand traps, where he can't use the strongest parts of his game. It is this strengths strategy that has helped him win so many tournaments.

TABLE 2: TWELVE STRENGTH-BUILDING STRATEGIES	
1. Courage	7. Perseverance
2. Interpersonal skills	8. Realism
3. Rationality	9. Desire for pleasure
4. Insight (leading to wisdom)	10. Perspective taking
5. Optimism (learned and otherwise)	11. Future mindedness
6. Honesty	12. Finding purpose and meaning

Here is another difference between positive psychology and the traditional view. The term *deviance* appears in both, but positive psychology turns it on its head. Traditionally, something that is deviant has been seen as negative. It deviates from the norm or expected, most often in a negative way. That's the deficiency-and-pathology interpretation. Using the positive psychology approach, the deviance to look for is positive: unexpected or abnormal behaviors or outcomes that are better, more favorable than the norm. These involve performances of unbelievable achievement, brilliance, and accomplishment. The positive deviance mind-set sets out to identify what is right with an individual or an organization, codify it, and then help others emulate it.

What a difference that outlook would make in the performance improvement field!

SPORT PSYCHOLOGY

Sport psychology has recently been expanded to include performance psychology regardless of the situation. The approach used here is very positive and has been successful not only for athletes but also for other performers (musicians, salespeople, speakers, and so on). The techniques of sport psychology include motivation, visualization, relaxation, quantitative measurement of performance for evaluation of improvement, positive reinforcement of strengths, recognition and rewards, and the building of the athlete's (performer's) self: self-esteem, self-confidence, self-worth, self-image, and self-control. It is what we call *head*coaching, and we have used these techniques repeatedly to turn ordinary performers into extraordinary performers.

In fact, because of the results we get using these positive sport psychology techniques with salespeople, executives, and athletes, some of our clients have likened our approach to alchemy. (You remember alchemy. It was an ancient science where they tried to turn lead into gold, or something very common into something precious.) We, as performance alchemists—our term—turn ordinary performers (lead) into extraordinary performers (gold). It is something our clients and their organizations definitely appreciate.

APPRECIATIVE INQUIRY

The appreciative inquiry approach to organizational improvement focuses on the strengths of individuals and their organizations. These strengths are then used to design a better future because they are positive building blocks. Appreciative inquiry also calls for total involvement and buy-in by the people affected by the new performance approach or culture. This also fits in with the Gallup work on focusing on people's strengths and doing whatever must be done to enhance and measurably improve those skills.

All these approaches invite managers and practitioners to look at HPT and performance improvement in a new way. Instead of finding out what is wrong and weak, look at what is strong and effective. Then develop ways to strengthen those strengths even more.

CUSTOMER SERVICE

Here's some fascinating research from another field: customer service and satisfaction. When companies conduct customer satisfaction surveys, they usually call for ratings from 1 to 5, with 5 indicating the respondent is extremely satisfied. The companies dissect their data so that each level of satisfaction is broken down. Then they look at the 1 and 2 ratings and devise intervention programs to raise the satisfaction levels of those customers.

And that is their mistake.

The research on loyalty clearly shows that it is next to impossible to raise the 1 and 2 ratings up to the 5 level. It is a waste of time and money to try. The research also shows that those customers who rate their satisfaction as a 3 or a 4 are most vulnerable. They are the people who are most likely to change suppliers or vendors if they receive a decent offer. So what can you do?

Here are some recommendations.

• Start with your extremely satisfied customers. Find out why they are so satisfied and then work hard and smart to keep them that way. You will receive your greatest profits from these customers, so work your hardest for them.

• Next, work on your 4 and 3 ratings. Consider their potential vulnerability to the offerings of your competitors and implement measures to prevent them from switching. Work to increase their satisfaction and loyalty. It is much easier to move a 4 or even a 3 up to a 5 (to make stronger customers even stronger) than it is to move the people at 1 or 2.

• As for these bottom two groups, forget about them. Cut them loose. Send them to a competitor. Don't waste your money, time, or energy on working to improve your relationship with them. They will never get up to the 5 level, and you will exhaust yourself trying to achieve that.

Now, how does this relate to performance improvement and enhancement in the workplace? It's a direct parallel. PI specialists tend to focus on finding the weakest performers and developing programs and interventions to help them get better. Yes, this is important, but these are not the people who are making the greatest contribution to their organizations. Better to spend the money, time, and energy on the top performers to make them even better since they contribute the most in productivity and profit.

It is the old 80/20 rule. In this version, 80 percent of contributions are made by 20 percent of performers (your level 5 performers). So the message is clear. Work with the top 20 percent to enhance their performance, and then work with the top 20 percent of the remaining 80 percent. Your performance 5s are where you will get the most bang for your buck. Meanwhile, your performance enhancement work with your 4s will show them you care about them and possibly prevent them from looking elsewhere for work. If there's anything left, save it for the 3s; the 1s and 2s belong elsewhere, and the sooner they realize it, the better off you and they will be.

POSITIVE CORE

As we said in Chapter 2, we began focusing on building a strong business core—an organizational approach resembling the fitness industry's emphasis on strengthening the core trunk muscles—more than twenty years ago. What we now call Positive CORE is based on the three areas described earlier in this chapter: positive psychology, sport psychology, and appreciative inquiry. With this approach, performance consultants can identify the core elements of individual performers that make them successful. It involves all the stakeholders of an organization in an effort to determine, define, and describe why the organization is where it is, why and how it functions as it does, and how it accomplishes what it does. Positive CORE then seeks to take the organization to another level of performance by making it more effective, productive, and successful in all areas by upgrading the current mental makeup, strengths, and motivational involvement of its individual performers.

The primary focus of Positive CORE is to identify successes and strengths rather than weaknesses and areas for improvement. The emphasis is placed on those strengths to create a multiplier effect so that they are increased and used to great advantage. The focus on the positive puts people in a better frame of mind, motivates them to continue to achieve, and creates a virtuous cycle of success seeking success.

The elements of the Positive CORE program are *confidence, outcomes, relationships,* and *engagement.* Each of these elements has several subcategories, as shown in Table 3.

The Positive CORE program results in performance improvement and performance enhancement because the performers buy in (become totally engaged), the focus on strengths and successes creates an ongoing positive atmosphere in which performance brings intrinsic rewards, and the organization finds it easier to implement the new performance culture because its people are more motivated. We discuss how you go about using the Positive CORE model and creating performance enhancement programs from it in the next four chapters.

TABLE 3: POSITIVE CORE ELEMENTS			
Confidence	*Outcomes*	*Relationships*	*Engagement*
Self-esteem	Goals, expectations, and reinforcements	Managers	Commitment
Strengths and talents	Measurement and evaluation	Friends and family	Emotions
Reinforcements and consequences	Results and returns: individuals, organizations, and society	Social, professional, and community contacts	Motivation and optimism

A SALES SUCCESS EXAMPLE

Implementation of Positive CORE is very easy to accomplish, especially in a sales environment. Sales success is easily measured, sales strengths are easily identified, and the psychobehavioral and motivational makeup of salespeople energizes them to constantly improve.

One organization with 175 salespeople found its sales growth stagnant. The individual reps were doing as well as in preceding years, but no one's share of the business was growing and the company was missing targets. As a result, the company began handing out negative consequences when reps did not meet daily goals and quarterly quotas. Still, performance did not improve, so the company put everyone through a standard sales training program. Again, no measurable increase in performance emerged. Obviously, what they were doing was not achieving their desired results.

We began the Positive CORE process with the sales managers. After we went through the four categories and their subcategories, as shown in Table 3, they had a clearer picture of the desired culture of the organization versus the one it had, the strengths of its performers and when the sales reps were at their best, who had the strongest relationships, who knew what was expected, how they became engaged in a task, and how the company and the individuals defined sales excellence. This profile was then described and taught to the rest of the sales force.

The initial results were encouraging as more sales reps started hitting their numbers. The Positive CORE approach was expanded to include work in the area of intrinsic motivation and development of higher levels of self-confidence. This was then followed by a tailored sales training program that taught all the reps the principles of psychobehavioral selling, influential communication (for both inside and outside the company), and the art of asking questions and listening. These skills enhanced the existing strengths of the sales force while simultaneously improving the CORE elements.

The result of the entire Positive CORE intervention was an increase in sales (the measurement program is still ongoing), an increase in the confidence of the sales reps as they engaged in more client-centered behaviors, and a change in the corporate culture from internally competitive to cooperative.

A PRACTICAL MANAGEMENT EXAMPLE

A large health care organization was having difficulty getting high performance from one of its departments. Each of the managers was well trained and dedicated to the organization, yet the department as a whole only met its base goals or performed slightly below baselines. This did not seem to make sense, so we were asked to determine how to turn this group into high performers.

We conducted Positive CORE interviews and determined that although all of the managers possessed the competencies to perform well, their performance objectives and expectations were not clearly spelled out. They were operating in the dark without a scorecard because they did not have quantifiable measurements (results) to shoot for. Plus, the department head was the strong, silent type—until something went wrong. Then he became very vocal and quick to point out the mistakes his people were making. This prevented the managers from being totally engaged in their performances.

Our interviews also uncovered the strengths of each of the managers. We suggested that they enumerate their strengths to the department head and develop their own performance objectives and results measurements and then present these to the department head. Since the managers now owned the performance activities, we predicted that their intrinsic motivation to perform and achieve would increase. And it did. We convinced the department head to let his managers run with the ball based on what they had created. His agreement helped the managers become even more engaged in their attempts to enhance current performance levels and improve whatever had to be improved.

The results were excellent. Within three months, the entire depart-
ment had exceeded previous performance metrics and its people were
consistently outperforming their colleagues in other departments. The
managers had taken ownership of their performance requirements and
were totally responsible and accountable for their own outcomes. This
led to constant engagement on their part, and each manager became a
cheerleader for other managers. We also coached the department head
to praise his people when appropriate and take a step back when he saw
them doing something wrong. We helped him understand that most
people know when they have made a mistake; pointing it out to them is
not always necessary. Plus, when all you do is point out mistakes with-
out ever giving praise or positive reinforcement, people will eventually
tune you out and stop listening. That is one of the reasons for the truth
of the maxim "People work for companies but they leave managers."

This Positive CORE approach led to increased performance across
the entire management team, including the department head. In a trickle-
down effect, employees' performance also increased. One year after implementation of this approach, the department was the most profitable in the
health care organization, the department head was promoted to senior vice
president, and several of the managers became department heads. All in
all, these were not bad results for everyone involved.

WHY POSITIVE CORE WORKS

Positive CORE works as an approach to performance improvement
because it focuses on the positive aspects of performance. You tell performers where they are already good or great and work with them to
make them even better. This motivates them to continue performing and
improving.

Here is what we are suggesting. Move from a deficit-and-pathology
model to a strengths-and-abundance model of performance. Move away
from the improvement-and-intervention approach, which is almost always

perceived as negative by the targeted performers, to an enhancement-and-engagement approach, where the performers build on their behavioral and emotional strengths. Then work to reinforce the performance of your top performers rather than struggling to raise that of your bottom performers.

It's human nature: we do most what we feel we do best. We perform what we get praised for more eagerly than what we get paid for. Remember that what gets rewarded gets repeated (both good and bad). So it is time for the HPT field to take a more positive approach to performance improvement and do the following:

- Keep the current models and systems and apply them in a new way
- Identify the strengths of all performers and work to improve them
- Focus on the top 20 percent of performers and make them even better
- Engage all performers through praise, reinforcement, and rewards
- Take a positive approach, focus on the positive, and stay positive

BENEFITS ON THE GROUND

Here are some ways that you, as a manager or a full-time HPT practitioner, will benefit from this new Positive CORE approach to performance enhancement. First, you will find it easier to work with your people or your performers as they will be more receptive to your suggestions. After all, you will no longer be pointing out where and why they are weak. You will be helping them advance their strengths. Second, economic buyers (CEOs, CFOs, and the rest of the C-level executives) will be more likely to fund your efforts because they will see the quantitative and qualitative results from their top performers.

Finally, you will enjoy your work more because you will have an easier path to do what you do best and enjoy most—helping people succeed. You will find that people are more receptive to you and that they will even welcome your efforts. You will also find that you can help them achieve measurable success, prove to them that they have been successful, and enhance your own self-esteem because you are able to help others.

When you combine the positive approach to performance enhancement and what it does for both the performer and the coach/manager with the level of results and the speed with which those results are achieved (thanks to the motivation and engagement of the performers), you have a whole new paradigm for performance improvement. You also have a way to communicate what you are offering and promising to achieve. To paraphrase an old commercial, try Positive CORE; you'll like it.

OUR CHALLENGE TO YOU

Our challenge here is a very simple one. Take a look at the PI efforts and interventions you have implemented in the past. Determine how successful each of them was and why a particular effort succeeded. Then review the elements of that successful intervention and identify how many of them related to this Positive CORE concept. Perhaps, without even knowing it, you have already begun using the strengths approach embodied by the Positive CORE approach and begun to get positive results. Once you view your past successes and failures this way, you'll further reinforce the power of the Positive CORE.

CONFIDENCE

The Power to Believe and Achieve

It started out like so many other coaching sessions we've been involved in. A person was doing well as a field performer, a management position opened up, and the company figured (as many companies mistakenly do) that the top performer would easily transition into a top manager.

Our new client had just been promoted to a senior management position because of her work in the field. Now she didn't know what she was going to do. All of a sudden, she had to attend meetings with other senior managers, write reports for the CEO and CFO to read, and create performance programs with accountabilities for her direct reports. Plus, she had the added stress of supervising people with whom she used to work on a peer level. She wondered how she was going to accomplish all

TABLE 4: POSITIVE CORE ELEMENTS			
Confidence	*Outcomes*	*Relationships*	*Engagement*
Self-esteem	Goals, expectations, and reinforcements	Managers	Commitment
Strengths and talents	Measurement and evaluation	Friends and family	Emotions
Reinforcements and consequences	Results and returns: individuals, organizations, and society	Social, professional, and community contacts	Motivation and optimism

that—she did not feel qualified to be in senior management. She was unsure of her abilities to perform at this level, and she did not believe she would be able to stick it out over time because of the new and different types of pressure she would be facing.

She came to us on her own, seeking help and paying for it out of her own pocket. She wanted to do well in her new job, but she just didn't think she had the skills or the mental outlook to succeed. It was our job to get her over the hump.

We conducted a series of interviews with the client, had her complete some profiles to give us deeper insight into her thoughts, emotions, and beliefs, and then had her role-play some specific managerial situations so we could observe her performance. As you've probably noticed, her initial problem was lack of confidence. The bottom line is that she did not believe in herself.

Now, here is where we differ from most coaches, based largely on our Positive CORE framework. Most coaches will work with a client like this to identify the sources of the thoughts and feelings that led to the lack of confidence. They will try to help the client work through those thoughts and feelings in the hope that it will resolve and overcome the problem. The trouble with this approach is that it borders on therapy, and that is not what coaching is about. Therapy is about resolving the past, and coaching is about helping people get to the next level—in other words, managing the future. This is especially true with our Positive CORE approach.

We worked with our client to identify all the areas in her life where she was successful. We discussed the thoughts and feelings she had when she was successful. Then we worked with her to simulate the transfer of those thoughts and feelings into her new job. When the client was confident that she could perform at a high level during our role-plays, we had her take her newfound confidence back to the job. We introduced one high-level management skill at a time as her confidence grew, and she was able to develop into a valuable member of the management team.

That is the power of the Positive CORE approach. The focus on positives, strengths, and successes speeds up the processes of skill acquisition, performance enhancement, and achievement. And it always increases a person's confidence.

CONFIDENCE BEGINS AT HOME

While the main focus of this book is on how managers can use Positive CORE to help their employees, managers must also strengthen their own Positive CORE. Therefore, at times we will speak directly to the manager in working through the Positive CORE approach.

Don't worry—we're not going to talk about your childhood and your upbringing and how they affect your confidence as an adult—as we said, that's therapy, and we're not in the therapy business. It is true that the past can have some effect on the present, but we don't dwell on it. And neither should you. What we mean by "confidence begins at home" is that it begins in your mind. It is part of your thought patterns and belief systems.

These, in turn, determine your self-esteem. But before we get into what your self-esteem is all about and how it affects your performance, and how you can use this segment of Positive CORE to enhance what you do and what your people do, let us introduce you to your new best friend: your own highly confident, peak-performing mind.

MEET YOUR NEW BEST FRIEND

Your peak-performing mind encompasses your thoughts, your emotions, your actions, your behaviors, and everything else that affects your performance. It starts with the mind but also includes the entire body, just as Positive CORE requires the involvement of the body in the performance of certain activities to achieve specific goals.

Take a minute to relax. Sit back and take a few long, slow, deep breaths. Feel the tension leaving your body—and your mind. Now picture a time when you did everything perfectly. It could be a sporting event, a sales presentation, or a performance review. It could be when you were playing a musical instrument, singing, dancing, making love, or doing anything else. Just get that picture in your mind and make sure it is very clear.

Keep imagining the scene and feel how smoothly everything flowed. It all occurred without your having to think about it. You just were there in the moment doing your thing. You were acting *unconsciously*, without thinking, and everything was going perfectly. In fact, when you started to think about it, the performance started to deteriorate. Your confidence started to wane when you began to think about what you were doing or how you were doing it.

Here's something fun to try. Next time you're participating in a sport, say, golf or tennis, and your opponent is just beating the pants off you, and nothing you do seems to work, ask your opponent, "Exactly what are you doing that is making you play so well?" You can be even more specific and ask the person if it's in the preparation, follow-through, or foot position. Ask him or her to think about it for a minute before answering. Your opponent will begin to think about the performance . . . and the performance will deteriorate. You may even win the match.

This works. People use it all the time, in athletic competition and in other activities. The point is that inappropriate thinking or excessive thought gets in the way of the highly confident, peak-performing mind.

UNDERSTANDING THE PEAK-PERFORMING MIND

Your peak-performing mind is the sum total of all your thoughts, emotions, behaviors, experiences, desires, and subconscious activity, coupled with a belief that you are the best you can be. It is the mind that is operating when the right and left hemispheres of your brain and your subconscious, conscious, and superconscious minds are functioning in perfect synchrony. Your brain waves are attuned to the activity at hand. The truth is that all the powers and capabilities of your mind are working together with your body to provide the peak performance, which usually results in your body being in the state of flow as you perform.

The mental state of a peak performer has been described as flowing, free from anxiety and tension, and extremely confident, with no competing or interfering thoughts. As an example, remember a time when everything you did went perfectly. You were just doing and being, not really thinking. In contrast, picture a basketball player going up for a jump shot but thinking, "Is my arm in the proper position? Can I make this shot? Will I come out of the game if I miss?" Or consider the golfer who before a drive, starts to think, "Now don't hit it into the rough. Stay out of the sand trap. Keep the club head up." Or think about one of your business presentations. If you were thinking things like, "What if I forget what I'm supposed to say? What if my slides don't work? Do I have any stains on my clothes?" you probably messed up the presentation unless you managed to get your mind out of this destructive cycle.

With too many thoughts running through your mind, your body doesn't have a chance to do its thing—which is perform naturally. The overactive mind can't do its job properly. *The peak-performing mind has now become the weak-performing mind.*

You can prevent this from happening by training your mind to relax, stay confident, and just do its thing. Start with a simple relaxation exercise, such as deep breathing. When you relax your body, your mind follows. This removes negative thoughts and makes you more receptive to positive suggestions that will build up your positive attitude, confidence, self-esteem, and belief system.

Another way to build your confidence and put your mind in the proper performance state is to use affirmations. Tell yourself positive things: "I am great. I am a capable performer. I am a successful person." Use these affirmations to get yourself into a highly motivated and confident state. Keep the affirmation statements in the present tense so you can experience them now. Then, when you have these feelings down pat and they turn into beliefs, you can develop affirmations to project yourself into the future, where you will be confident and perform well. In fact, the skill of visualization is nothing more than imagining the future as the present in a positive manner. In your mind, you achieve that peak performance and always win.

> *In one program we conducted, we had a triathlete vividly describe his best-ever Iron Man performance. We asked him to describe it using all his senses and to paint the most realistic (word) picture possible for the audience. He was so into his description, he started to relive all the positive feelings and emotions he had experienced during the race. He was getting very excited. His description was so good that the audience started to have similar feelings. They shared the joy, the elation, the chills, the desire to win, and the overwhelming feeling of accomplishment when the triathlon was completed. When he finished, they applauded as if everyone was actually at the finish line.*

You must use this same vividness to put your mind in the right state. Include all the sights, sounds, smells, tastes, and feelings of the previous peak performance. (Pay attention to how you start to feel all over when you relive this experience. You'll be amazed at how tall you get—and how your confidence level soars.)

If you can't visualize a past peak performance, create one in your mind. Act "as if" and become a peak performer. That's what all of us really do anyway. We pretend to be something and then, with enough practice, that pretense becomes a reality. Just look at children as they play pretend and copy role models. That's how they get so good at what they do and who they are. You should do it, too.

Remember, you don't have to be an athlete to achieve this. We work with professional speakers, trainers, executives, teachers, and many others to help them achieve peak performance in their line of work. So mentally make yourself a peak performer to put your mind in the proper state for whatever you have to do. Once you've imagined yourself successfully performing, go out and actually perform. Don't judge your actions and don't be critical. Just do it and notice the outcome. The less critical you are of yourself, the better you'll perform—and the more confidence you will develop for future performances.

A HIGHER-LEVEL PEAK-PERFORMING MIND

Here's a bonus tip for achieving a higher level of performance and confidence. Use the acronym FIRE. It stands for *focus, imagine, relax,* and *execute.*

The first thing you do is *focus* on your target. Create a laserlike focus and stick with it. This arouses your desire and commitment to achieve a goal. Plus, when you are totally focused on something, your mind and your body will do everything possible to get you exactly what you want.

Think back to a time when you were totally focused on achieving something. Weren't you confident, motivated, and committed to getting what you wanted? Didn't you do everything in your power to achieve your goal? Wasn't your mind geared to guiding you to a top-level performance that would help you achieve your goal?

This is the power of focus. When businesses have a focus, they succeed where their competitors fail. Focused corporations do well;

unfocused ones do poorly. Athletes who focus on their sport do well; unfocused athletes never seem to make the grade. Business professionals who are focused on their goals and achievements perform significantly better than do those who lack focus. Stay focused on your target. Always keep it in sight.

Next, *imagine* yourself succeeding. Do this before you get involved in your task. You must constantly use imagery to take you to a higher level of achievement. Visualize, fantasize, dream, imagine, paint pictures, make mental movies, or whatever. Do what you must to get clear, solid pictures in your mind of what you want to achieve and how you're going to go about achieving it. Remember that the mind (and the nervous system) doesn't differentiate between a real memory and an imagined (visualized) event—they feel the same as you think about them. So if you create pictures in your mind, your mind will feel them as actual perceptions of what is happening in your world—and respond accordingly—as will your body.

Therefore, when you envision peak performance, you respond with peak performance. *Imagine* the possibilities.

After you've imagined yourself performing at your peak, and before you actually go out to perform, *relax.* You're still intently focused on what you want. You're just going to achieve it without tensing up. Every performance goes better when the mind and the body are in a state of relaxed alertness. Your conscious and subconscious minds work together to take you to a higher level. Relaxed alertness makes everything move in slow motion, makes your targets bigger, makes fatigue disappear, makes your confidence soar, and moves your peak performance to a higher level. So *relax.*

The last part of the FIRE acronym is *execute;* execute your actions. This means you perform as if you were just automatically running off your motor program, much like a computer program, with no outside interference. The program just starts and naturally runs to completion.

Your mind and your body already know how to execute your desired activity (sales presentation, sports move, speech, music; it doesn't matter) perfectly. So it's up to you to let them do their thing. When you execute properly, you can't help but excel. It's when you try to think too much, when you let your mind get too active in the process, that the performance is less than optimal.

Now that you've achieved a higher level of performance, you can store the behaviors, thoughts, emotions, and feelings in your memory for playback at a later date. You can rehearse for new situations by reliving old ones. You can transfer skills and feelings from previous peak experiences, using your imagination, to future peak experiences before they happen. You can use this database of success to help you keep your confidence at a high level.

It's really all up to you. Do you want to be a run-of-the-mill, average performer who disappears in a crowd, or do you want people to consider you a confident peak performer, someone they can count on for top quality at all times? Someone they can get the ball to for the last shot of the game, someone to put in the batter's box in the bottom of the ninth, to get onstage and deliver a speech to motivate a team at work, to turn the company around in a time of crisis; the list goes on. We strongly believe that everyone would like to be in the peak performer class. Now, knowing what you know about the peak-performing mind and how to develop, nurture, and maintain that mind-set, you can be a peak performer all the time.

YOUR SELF-ESTEEM PROFILE

When you are a peak performer, your confidence level is at the top of the scale and it is easy to maintain a high level of self-esteem, one of the main components of building confidence. In this section, we discuss two other areas that hinge on self-esteem—self-motivation and belief systems. But first, complete the simple assessment in Exercise 1 to help you get on the road to higher confidence. Follow the instructions for taking it and for scoring it. We have used it successfully with thousands of clients to identify their self-esteem level and to show how their self-esteem affects their

Exercise 1: SELF-ESTEEM ASSESSMENT

Success in any area of life is closely linked to your self-esteem. Respond to each statement using the scale below. Write the appropriate number (from 1 to 5) on the line preceding each item.

Never	Almost Never	Sometimes	Almost Always	Always
1	2	3	4	5

___ 1. I am in charge of my life.

___ 2. I avoid taking on new projects because I fear I might fail.

___ 3. When I make a mistake, I get over it quickly and get on with my life.

___ 4. I wish I could be more like someone else.

___ 5. I believe I can do just about anything I set my mind to do.

___ 6. In situations where I feel uncomfortable, I focus on people's negative attributes.

___ 7. I use my full name when I'm introduced to new people.

___ 8. When I screw up, I berate myself or put myself down in some way.

___ 9. I try to focus on the positive attributes of every situation.

___ 10. When things work out well for me, I attribute it to luck or circumstances.

___ 11. I respect other people's opinions.

___ 12. I am envious of people who are more successful than I am.

___ 13. I look for ways to help others.

___ 14. I believe that when I'm criticized for something, it's a personal attack on me.

___ 15. I am constantly trying to improve myself.

___ 16. I am more interested in what I have to say to other people than in what they're saying to me.

___ 17. I like challenges because they cause me to stretch my abilities.

___ 18. I have difficulty accepting a compliment.

___ 19. I believe in myself.

___ 20. I wonder if I'm worthy of success.

Scoring the Self-Esteem Assessment

There are two ways to score this assessment. The first method helps you identify your general level of self-esteem. The second method helps you pinpoint specific areas of strength and areas that require work on your part.

The first way to score the assessment is to look at the odd-numbered statements and add up your rankings for those statements. Then look at the even-numbered statements. These are low-self-esteem statements and are scored in reverse, so if you rated yourself a 1, which is good on these statements, you would actually score a 5. Similarly, if you rated yourself a 5, you would score a 1. So, on the even-numbered statements, reverse the scoring then add them up and add that score to the total from the odd-numbered statements. The best score possible is 100. Anything less than an 80 requires work on your part to improve your self-esteem.

The second way to score the assessment is to keep in mind the odd and even directions of the statements. Issues in any odd-numbered statement you rate a 3 or less require work. For the even-numbered statements, ratings of 3, 4, or 5 require work on that item.

Of course, you can use both scoring systems, as we do. Then we are able to help our clients work on their self-esteem as a whole as well as on individual areas.

---

performance. This assessment will give you insight into where you are now and where you want to get to with your self-esteem.

SELF-ESTEEM AND SELF-MOTIVATION

In Chapter 1 we discussed the difference between intrinsic and extrinsic motivation, and how both are necessary at specific times. With intrinsic motivation, a performer does the job for the sake of the job and the satisfaction that is derived from accomplishment. Extrinsic motivation moves that performance forward based on rewards, reinforcements, and consequences. Both types of motivation combined form your self-motivation, which is closely related to self-esteem and confidence. When you complete Exercise 2, you'll easily be able to see how your self-motivation affects your self-esteem related to any performance.

Exercise 2: SELF-MOTIVATION QUESTIONNAIRE

Answer the following questions in the space provided to help you determine your self-motivation.

What motivates you to perform?

_____

_____

What motivates you to perform *well?*

_____

_____

What *holds you back* from performing well?

_____

_____

What *causes* you to perform poorly?

_____

_____

What are your three greatest fears in relation to performing on your job?

_____

_____

What are your personal strengths? (We'll get to these later in this chapter.)

_____

_____

What do you have to do to be the top producer in your company?

_____

_____

What reinforcements do you prefer when you do well?

_____

_____

What consequences are you willing to accept for not performing well?

_____

_____

Who is primarily responsible for your success as a performer?

_____

_____

SELF-ESTEEM AND BELIEF SYSTEMS

It is one thing to talk about building up your self-esteem and another to actually believe that you have high self-esteem. Your beliefs in any area guide your thoughts, behaviors, and interactions with other people. That is why you must truly *believe* that you are worthy of having a high level of self-esteem. To help you, we have created a "belief-generating acronym" that will help you elevate your self-esteem, increase your confidence, and basically build a better life, both professionally and personally. It is based on seven values that most people say they have or would like to have and that, over time, have resulted in exceptional levels of achievement. The first letters of these seven values spell out GET RICH:

- **Generosity:** Your willingness to give of yourself to others in your company and your community, in terms of both money and time and effort, will make you feel better about yourself. When you feel better about yourself, you are more positive in everything you do. The result is greater self-esteem.

- **Empathy:** When you understand what other people are feeling in certain situations, and you can control your emotions and communicate your understanding, you will make them feel better about themselves. This, in turn, will make you feel better about yourself, which raises your self-esteem.

- **Trust:** Trust, liking, and credibility are the real TLC of the world. When you trust people, they trust you back. When you do what you say you will when you say you will do it, people believe in you and feel they can trust you. It is wonderful to know that people trust you and have confidence in you because you are a person of your word. This raises your self-esteem.

- **Respect:** Everyone craves respect. People will do almost anything, both positive and negative, to get the respect of someone else. When you automatically and instantly respect someone, and show it, that person will respect you in return. Respecting people, making them feel appreciated and important, is one of the greatest gifts you can give to others to boost their self-esteem, and yours as well.

- **Integrity:** Integrity and honesty are closely tied together, along with consistency and credibility. Be aboveboard at all times. Tell the truth, don't scam people, and give people the benefit of the doubt. Be a person who is beyond reproach. People will admire you for your high level of integrity, and this will increase your self-esteem.

- **Commitment:** What are you passionate about? What do you have a desire to do and achieve? What motivates you to carry on in the face of obstacles? This is what we are talking about when we say you must make a commitment. Confidence and commitment go together. The confident person commits to achieving a goal and persists until it is achieved. The entire sequence is designed to increase your self-esteem.

- **Happiness:** You wake up every day with a choice of being happy or unhappy. Happiness is based on your interpretation of the world around you. No one makes you happy. Some people think that having a lot of money will make them happy, but that is not necessarily true. Many wealthy people are very unhappy, and many people who do not have much money are very happy. Happiness is an emotion. The more times you are happy or experience happiness, and the higher your level of happiness, the higher your self-esteem will be.

The key here is to understand that you will increase your self-esteem if you just GET RICH. You will subsequently improve your performance and receive more positive feedback and reinforcement. This will cycle back on itself to give you even greater self-esteem and more confidence in what you do. Who knows? Your self-esteem and confidence levels may get so high that you'll undertake new tasks and become an even more valued performer in your organization. And think what will happen if you transfer these thoughts, feelings, and actions to your employees. Everyone will be a stronger employee and performer. And won't that be great for everyone?

BUILDING EMPLOYEE STRENGTHS AND TALENTS

The human resource processes of recruiting, hiring, training, and retaining employees have morphed into the arena of talent management. Companies create a talent profile and then attempt to hire to fit that profile. They use the standard approaches of targeted selection, behavioral interviewing, and selection inventories. Then they use a systematic decision-making approach to finalize their hire, create a performance management program to ensure the new hire is well trained and coached, and then provide for various evaluative sessions to determine the performer's strengths and weaknesses. While the talent management concept has its merits, companies are still losing employees to competitors or even to entrepreneurship. Something else must be added to the mix to keep those employees and make sure they are performing at their peak.

That something comes from positive psychology and work by the Gallup organization in a branch of the field called *strengths psychology*. Work in strengths psychology is focused on identifying the physical, mental, and emotional attributes of top performers who are completing tasks or activities in areas where they are strongest. For example, someone who is good with details and numbers will be a better performer in an accounting or computer job than in a field sales job. Someone who is excellent with people should be out front with the people and not in some back-office job. This is playing to their strengths. And when you consistently play to people's strengths, they become much more confident. This confidence translates into higher levels of performance, a willingness to take on additional and more difficult tasks, and an increase in self-esteem.

We do a great deal of work with sales organizations. One of the expected behaviors of a sales rep is to make outbound telephone calls. Companies develop scripts for their salespeople and assume that since many sales organizations became successful through teleselling, their salespeople should do the same with the scripts they have available to them. The problem is that many salespeople are more effective in person than they are on the phone. If that's the case, why would you have someone spend hours on the phone, where they are weak, and not out with people, where they are strong?

Once we help our clients determine the strengths of their sales reps, we redesign the reps' work tasks to reflect those strengths. The ones who are better at socializing are expected to attend meetings, network at functions, and go out on appointments. Those who are better on the phone are expected to be in the office making those calls. The result for the organization is that the salespeople are happier playing to their strengths and their performance always improves.

STRENGTHS, TALENTS, AND GOAL ACHIEVEMENT

Managers know that they must work with employees to set goals for job performance. These goals must be in line with the company's business objectives as well as with the performer's strengths. When the goals mirror the strengths and talents of a performer, that performer is much more motivated and inclined to work hard on achieving the goals. When a goal is in an area in which the performer does not possess the strength or talent for success at the task, then the performer retires on the job, goes through the motions, or emotionally quits (what we refer to as disengaging). No one wants that situation in their organization, nor do they want to manage people who are psychologically not there.

So, as a manager who desires a high-performing workforce, it is your job to identify the strengths and talents of your people, set goals with them that play to those strengths and talents, and provide a work environment that will help them achieve those goals. Think of the problems that occur if you provide the opposite. No one wants to come to work bad day after bad day. No one wants to put forth the effort and energy to achieve at high levels when they are not allowed to use their strengths and talents. And no one wants to work for a manager or company that doesn't care about them. That's why you must identify, focus on, and play to the strengths and talents of your people.

NOT KNOWING YOUR OWN STRENGTHS

By now, you realize that we are all for an extensive focus on strengths. This is critical to every performer's success—and to your success as a manager. It is in everyone's best interest to identify and bring out the strengths of each performer. Yet some people are blind to their own strengths and talents. How many times have you heard the phrase "latent potential" or "late bloomer"? This means that someone somehow was able to display a skill at a high level of performance at a point in life when no one expected him or her to do so.

Think back to Grandma Moses, who was in her eighties when she discovered that she was a great artist. Or to Colonel Sanders, who became an entrepreneurial icon in his sixties and remained so for years after that. Or to athletes who started late and became superstars after only a few years of playing a sport. How did they tap into these strengths and all of a sudden bring them out?

What makes people late bloomers? We have discovered three primary reasons. The first is that some people simply don't know what their strengths are in a particular field or situation. This may seem silly, but many people are truly unaware of what they do well. They may have been pushed into a career or life path and, for whatever reasons, never sought to change it. For example, how many boys are told they should be doctors, lawyers, or even pro athletes? Many children hear things like this over and over. What happens to the boy in this situation who has talent as an artist, a dancer, or a businessperson? And what about the girl who has an affinity for science, math, and engineering but is steered toward traditional "female" careers because girls are not supposed to be strong in those areas? Why do parents and teachers sometimes neglect these potential strengths in favor of the more expected ones? Could it be that as adults (parents, teachers, managers) we tend to push people into the areas we know best and are most comfortable with? Your answers to these questions will tell you a great deal about why people are sometimes unaware of their strengths. They haven't had an opportunity to find out what they are good at.

Another reason people don't know or display their strengths is that they are afraid they will be seen as showing off. They hide their strengths or play different roles in hopes of being more accepted by certain groups or individuals. Some people are great singers, yet they do not share their talent because they don't want to show off. Some people are great artists, but they don't draw or paint because they are afraid people will compare them with the masters. And others who are great organizational performers in the field act like they can't manage others so they won't be promoted. They don't want to stand out above the crowd and risk losing acceptance. As consultants, we often have to work hard to help people identify and show their strengths so we can help them increase their confidence and performance levels.

The third reason people don't know their strengths is because they don't recognize their accomplishments. Many people we work with say they have not been very successful in their lives. They think success has to be some big thing like saving a life, making a lot of money, owning and running a successful megacorporation, or something monumental like that. We disagree with these perspectives. Success is anything you have accomplished at any time in your life. You were successful when you

---

Exercise 3: REAL-LIFE SUCCESS

Here's what we want you to do: Think of a recent success. Get it clearly in your mind. Consider the few external factors that affected you and that were involved in that success. Then focus on the internal factors that led to your success. Think about your behaviors, your feelings, your thoughts, your preparation for the event, your awareness of the situation, your persistence or desire to succeed. Get these clear in your mind for this particular success and then think of another similar successful act on your part. Go through the same process and you'll probably find many of the same elements. These are your strengths coming to the forefront. The more you repeat this exercise, the more you'll uncover your strengths and how many times you've really been successful.

---

learned how to walk, ride a bike, drive a car, love someone besides yourself, work with others, write a book, give a speech, play a sport, play an instrument, and do countless other things small and large. Success is accomplishment, and the level of that accomplishment is only a matter of degree. Try Exercise 3 to see what we mean.

Once you've got the hang of it, try this exercise with your individual employees. By doing so, you will help them find both their successes and their strengths. Once they identify their strengths, they may want to display them in appropriate situations.

Performance improvement will inevitably follow. Remember the maxims: *Do what you love and the money will follow. Be passionate about what you do. Your strengths will help you survive, thrive, and flourish.* Whatever the cliché, the sentiment is the same. Instead of fixing flaws and doing more of what seems difficult, you and your people need to find ways to stop doing what you don't like to do or you're not good at and start doing what you like and what you are good at. The more you do this, the more confident you will become. The same is true for any performer. And someone who becomes more confident will get significantly better results for every action. You have to do this for yourself—and your people. You must help them do what they are best at and then repeat those behaviors. One way you can do this is by providing the proper reinforcements and consequences when your people perform.

CONSEQUENCES AND REINFORCEMENTS

It's simple to build confidence in your people: Have them do what they do well, give them positive reinforcements and rewards when they achieve their results and accomplish their goals, and then let them do it all over again. Simple, effective, and repeatable. This approach guarantees success in raising the confidence levels of your employees. It also helps create winning streaks. People who are confident in what they do and who see the results of their efforts (rewards and reinforcements) tend to continue to perform well in those areas. High levels of confidence and high levels of self-esteem start to cycle back on each other, with one producing the other in a seemingly endless virtuous loop. Performers go through cycles of high performance sustained over a period of time. They also go through what we call "psychles" of sustained high confidence and high self-esteem during these times. The only problem is that no one can sustain these high levels of performance and confidence over an extended period. So it is up to managers and coaches to help people move through decreased-performance cycles and psychles until they can once again achieve those high levels.

Unfortunately, it is also simple to hinder confidence and performance, and sometimes managers do it unknowingly. No matter how desirable it is for people to focus on their strengths and constantly perform well, they often have to perform tasks that are outside their comfort or skill zone. When this happens, they don't always achieve their goals. It's not that they are being set up for failure, it's just that the job requires them to employ skills they either do not yet have or have not yet developed to a high level. So they perform and they miss their mark. Many managers give positive reinforcement even though it is not deserved, out of the mistaken notion that they should always be positive and never talk about or bring up consequences for poor performance. But as long as people do what they do without truthful feedback, they will unwittingly continue to perform at unacceptable levels. Another problem is that people may get bored because they are performing a task that is not part of their strengths repertoire, but they think they are good at it because their manager has been telling them so. The mind-set becomes, *If I do this so well and it is so dull and easy, why should I put any effort into it? My manager is happy with what I'm doing, so why try harder?*

TRUTH OR CONSEQUENCES?

Managers need to work to maintain the delicate balance of getting people to play to their strengths, reinforcing their performance in such a way as to build up their confidence and skill levels simultaneously, while providing consequences for their actions that can be used as learning tools to improve future performance. This is a difficult situation for a manager. You don't want to shake people's confidence by telling them they did something poorly or by punishing them in some way for not achieving the goal. Yet you know that the performance was not up to par. You have a multitude of choices as to how to handle this situation. What do you do?

You can soft-sell the performance and tell the employee that it could have been better. You can use the Oreo cookie approach and say something nice, tell the employee what was wrong and how it should be improved, and then say something nice again. However, when you use this approach repeatedly, your people come to expect something bad to follow anything good that you might say. You can dole out punishments for the poor performance and tell the employee (or yell at the employee) that the performance was not up to expectations. This fear approach may work for a while, but eventually it loses its power because employees stop caring or become content to wait until the storm blows over.

Many managers avoid confrontation because they don't want their people thinking of them as cold and uncaring. They want their employees to like them so that everyone in the department can work well together. You can also let everything slide and hope the performance improves the next time. This is similar to "ostrich management," where you put your head in the sand and hope things will be different when you pull it out later. Or you can be truthful and work with the employee to examine the performance and determine what happened, what should have happened, and what is expected next time.

This last approach is obviously the preferred one, and it will build the employee's confidence the most and the fastest for a couple of reasons. First, you are involving the employee in the evaluation. All employees want input into their own performance evaluation or feedback session. The more involved they are in the evaluation process, the more engaged they become for the next time—a pattern that forms the main topic of Chapter 7. Second, you are working with the employee to develop the consequences for a poor or less-than-expected performance. When people have a role in determining their own consequences, they are more likely to own the performance and its outcomes. They know what is expected and what they will receive for a job well done or poorly done, and they will be confident that they can accomplish the goal. If the consequences for a performance outcome are negative, they will not be as hurtful since the employee was involved in determining them before the performance occurred.

And that is an important point. Make certain that every performer knows the consequences (either rewards or punishments) related to the whole range of performance outcomes before the performance begins. This means that you no longer have to worry about truth or consequences since you both will be involved in truth *and* consequences.

REWARDS AND REINFORCEMENTS

When we work with colleagues to help them build the confidence of their employees, we like to bring up an old maxim that has been proven countless times in psychology laboratories, organizational settings, and schools: *What gets rewarded or reinforced gets repeated.* It is basic psychology that was tested with Skinner's pigeons and Pavlov's dogs. When a performer believes a reward will be received after doing something (or doing something well) and then actually *receives* a reward, the performer will repeat the performance. The question then becomes, Is the performance repeated because it was intrinsically satisfying to the performer or to receive the reward again? It is not our intent to get into a psychological debate on the merits of intrinsic versus extrinsic motivation and how they affect performance. We bring up the subject because many savvy managers have learned how to use extrinsic reinforcers and rewards to build people's confidence so they can begin doing the job for the intrinsic satisfaction that comes from doing that job well. So, for our purposes in building our Positive CORE model, we recommend that you use both intrinsic and extrinsic rewards to help people build their confidence levels.

Types of Rewards—Managers have traditionally used three types of rewards to build the confidence levels of their employees: pay, opportunity, and benefits. Pay is money. While many people think that money motivates everyone, that is not actually true. Money is important, but not to the extent that managers and organizations tend to think it is. In fact, many personnel surveys have shown that while management thinks money is the primary motivator or reinforcer, employees rank money down around fifth or sixth in a list of ten motivators. Employees want more intangible things like job satisfaction, job enrichment, and knowing the impact their job has on the people and communities they serve. The point here is that managers must consider both the tangible and intangible rewards that people prefer.

This leads us to the concept of opportunity as a reinforcement technique. Opportunity means different things to different people. To some it can mean job security, while to others it can mean a promotion or a raise. Opportunity can also be in the form of succession planning or a variety of career advancement paths. The simplest way to find out how opportunity can be used as a reward is to ask the individual performers what they prefer. The same is true for job-related benefits. People may want more vacation time, flex time, family time, insurance coverage, or any of a variety of other things in lieu of financial rewards. For one client we worked with several years ago in Florida, a team was given the choice of a financial reward of $300 or tickets for four to Walt Disney World for the day.

More people took the tickets as the reward for performing well than took the money. They viewed it as an extra benefit.

Given that you have three types of organizational rewards, how can you use them in the best manner possible? First, it's clear that rewards and reinforcements are used to shape behavior. You can reinforce appropriate behavior and outcomes or you can withhold reinforcement and rewards for behavior that leads to inappropriate outcomes. In either case, the idea is to shape the behavior of employees to generate the desired level of performance. You can also work to get this performance through the types of rewards you offer. These can be tangible, in the form of cash, or intangible, in the form of words of encouragement or recognition. Some people prefer tangible rewards such as money, plaques, certificates, trips, and clothing, to name a few things, while others prefer a compliment, a note, a pat on the back, or just a word of encouragement. The best way to find out what types of rewards and reinforcements people prefer is to ask them.

Whatever type they prefer, you will find that they want rewards that satisfy their basic needs, appear to be fair and equitable for everyone concerned, and fit their own individual motivations and desires. Basic needs include things like safety, security, housing, food, and the like. In fact, in the mid-1990s, one of the most popular rewards for salespeople was gift certificates to restaurants. Not cash. Just the certificate for the food. Isn't it strange how some things motivate people to perform better?

Fairness and equity are strictly in the minds of the people receiving the rewards. No one wants to get cheated or slighted. Just as the phrase "a full day's pay for a full day's work" sets out the basic agreement of employment, people want an equal reward for an equal performance compared to what their colleagues receive. No one wants to get less than someone else for accomplishing the same thing. People will be willing to take more, but no one wants to get less. So remember to consider this effect on an employee's future confidence levels related to future performance. Along these same lines, you must consider individual motivations. What makes each employee tick and what does that employee want? How can you create the environment that helps each person build confidence, grow as an employee, and achieve high levels of performance?

How Personalized Rewards Have Helped—Here are two examples of how personalized rewards and reinforcers helped a client help a team develop greater confidence and perform better.

We worked with a sales team of twelve reps who'd been offered a $25 cash incentive (on top of the regular commissions and bonuses) to achieve certain numbers. This did nothing to improve performance. When the team's manager called us, we suggested he interview each rep and find out specifically what that rep wanted in the way of a reward. He did so and found out that the majority of his team wanted a $25 gift card from American Express. He did not understand why they wanted that instead of the same amount in cash. We explained to him that it was a matter of personal control. The reps could hold on to the gift cards, collect several of them, and buy what they wanted when they wanted. The cash was usually spent immediately, sometimes even to pay bills. So we advised him to give out the gift cards and track performance. In two months, performance had significantly improved.

In another case, we worked with a family-owned business with more than a hundred employees that was suffering from excessive turnover. The company had started offering cash incentives for people to stay six months or more, but the results weren't satisfactory. We suggested they ask employees what would keep them on the job for a year. They did this and found out that only 10 percent of the employees wanted cash rewards. Most of the people wanted management to be more positive when they communicated with the staff.

Up until we became involved, it turned out, most of the managers had only talked to employees to tell them they had done something wrong. It was rare that a manager said something positive, gave an employee a pat on the back, or showed appreciation for a job well done in some other way. This led to a decrease in employees' level of confi-dence, since they didn't think they could do the job well enough to receive a compliment. When the negativity built up to a level that they could not stand anymore, they left the company. So we suggested that managers start looking for the good in their people and work to catch them doing things right. Then, when they found the positives, they were to compliment the performers on the spot. We even had the company print up little sticky notes that said "Job Well Done" and required the managers to give them to employees whenever the employees achieved a desired outcome.

Confidence levels began to improve—and along with those confi-dence levels, performance improved and turnover decreased. Now, with people staying on the job longer, profitability also increased because not as much money had to be allocated to recruitment and replacement.

The bottom line here is that individualized rewards, reinforcements, and consequences actually increase employees' confidence, involvement, and subsequent performance. Take a look at your own life. How do you feel you are going to perform in a situation when you are highly confident as opposed to when you are unsure of yourself? Your confidence leads you to a superior performance and your lack of confidence results in a poorer performance. Anyone who lacks confidence in a job and has to repeat that job too often will eventually leave the job. It takes a wise manager to make sure the performance environment is right, the reinforcements are right, and the consequences are right so that every performer has the confi-dence to do a great job.

OUR CHALLENGE TO YOU

Confidence is a critical factor in positive performance outcomes. Athletes who are confident win more often. Artists who are confident produce bet-ter art. Educators who are confident produce better students. And employees who are confident produce better outcomes.

Here is our challenge: Take the time to meet with all your employees. Give them the self-esteem assessment in this chapter. Interview them to determine their perceived strengths and talents. Ask others for opinions on your people's strengths and talents. Then ask your people what they prefer as rewards and reinforcements for a job well done, as well as what consequences they expect when they miss their goals.

Create a comprehensive file on each employee. Refer to this file on a regular basis when you deal with employees. Then, whenever the situation arises, give employees the type of reinforcement they each prefer, show them that you appreciate their efforts, and determine whether the consequences are positive or negative. Finally, ask the employees to rate their confidence for the next time that task comes up. Track all these results in your file. You will be pleasantly surprised at how the confidence levels of your people improve along with their performance levels.

— *FIVE* —

OUTCOMES

Results, Returns, and Reinforcement

The most consistent thing about PI is the inconsistency that surrounds it. Companies spend millions of dollars on training programs, software purchases, and e-learning implementations and then fail to successfully implement the PI process. The failure and program discard rates are constantly published in various PI publications and on Web sites, yet the prognosis for PI still remains very positive. Experts agree that corporate spending on PI will continue to increase in the next few years.

This presents an interesting dilemma. Why would companies jump on the bandwagon knowing that their colleagues and competitors may be failing? Why would professional organizations promote the value of workplace learning and performance and implementing various PI technologies

TABLE 5: POSITIVE CORE ELEMENTS			
Confidence	*Outcomes*	*Relationships*	*Engagement*
Self-esteem	Goals, expecta-tions, and rein-forcements	Managers	Commitment
Strengths and talents	Measurement and evaluation	Friends and family	Emotions
Reinforcements and consequences	Results and returns: individuals, organizations, and society	Social, professional, and community contacts	Motivation and optimism

when the majority of interventions are not accomplishing what they are supposed to accomplish? And why would the experts continue to tout the benefits of PI when so many of their clients (internal and external) are not achieving desired results?

ORGANIZATIONAL TRAPS

We are often called into a company to help its leaders determine why their highly rated training programs are not yielding results in terms of performance improvement. The company has an entire curriculum of programs that the employees attend. The employees evaluate each program, the instructor, the materials, and anything else the training or HR department can think of. And the ratings are good. High marks for the course, the instructor, the materials—even the food and the facility get good marks.

Yet behavior never changes. Performance shows no discernible improvement over time. Nor is there any measurable improvement in business results or impact outside the organization. So we are asked to figure out the problem.

MEASUREMENT MISALIGNMENT

Several problems can exist, but the first and most important is that the measurement is wrong and that is why the company can't determine if it is truly getting the results it is seeking. When you measure the things we mentioned (course, instructor, materials), you are measuring processes, not accomplishments. And as important as the processes are, they are not and should never be your final measurement. You must develop specific measures for the outcomes you are looking for. These measures must be objective, quantifiable, and reportable. They must link the learning (or coaching) to changes in behavior that lead to enhancements or improvements in performance, which then lead to more positive business results. And that is what we help companies do.

MYTHS AND TRUTHS OF PI

We also find that companies encounter problems because they are living the seven myths of PI: seven traps that companies fall into that cause them to not achieve the results they expect. And because the company has bought into these myths, the individual performers buy into them also. Take a look at the seven myths and their related truths. Consider how they apply to your company, your department, and your employees. Then ask yourself what you are going to do about exchanging these myths for realities.

MYTH 1: PI is about managing data, systems, and processes.

TRUTH: PI, as it exists today, really is more about managing data (causal analysis, gap analysis, research, and so on) than about managing people—and that's precisely the problem. It is full of theories about how to collect data, massage data, and interpret data to determine the proper intervention. This focus on data management leads to the same type of behavior where employees are concerned: managers attempt to control employees as if they were data, and then they wonder why they are not getting positive results. Spending too much time on the management-and-control aspect of PI is a prescription for failure.

Performers do not want to be controlled. They want to be advised, coached, and guided, but they do not want to be told what to do. Yet many current PI approaches focus on that. Companies do not and cannot manage their people. Performers want to manage themselves. It gives them the all-important sense of being in control, rather than being controlled. If companies would focus more on the relationship aspect of PI than on its theory and data aspects, they would be more successful.

MYTH 2: Data analysis is the key to success.

TRUTH: Analysis is merely another way to slice and dice the research and data. Sure, it can give you unique pictures of performance outcomes and maybe even performer habits. But it cannot give you what the performers want and need: true personalization.

Analysis can determine exactly what a performer has done in the past and offer some recommendations for interventions that might intrigue the performer and motivate him or her to do better. But is that truly what the performer wants?

Performers want the human touch. They want to talk with and get their performance problem resolved or improved by a real person. Analysis is important to PI success, but anyone who thinks that constantly gathering and analyzing data takes the place of communicating with performers is sadly mistaken. If you really must do analysis, do a people analysis. Find out what makes your people tick, what gets them up in the morning and keeps them awake at night. Learn what they really want from the job, what they want to accomplish, and how they want to contribute. Once you do this, you can dig into the data.

MYTH 3: Technology breeds and builds relationships.

TRUTH: This myth is closely related to Myth 2. Companies that have the latest and greatest performance technologies (EPSS—electronic performance support systems—for example) do not always have a great relationship with their performers. The philosophy of "if you build (or buy) it, they will come" is totally inappropriate and misleading. We know of companies that have spent millions of dollars on technology, only to leave that software sitting on the shelf. We know of other companies that have spent similar sums trying to learn about their performers (usually through online testing and profiling), only to fail miserably in their quest.

Having great technology does not guarantee that performers will perform better for you, nor does it guarantee that you will truly know your performers any better than if you had lesser technology. Always remember that technology has nothing to do with relationships—*people do.*

MYTH 4: PI success comes from full-scale implementation of a performance improvement process.

TRUTH: This myth explains why many PI implementations fail to achieve their desired or expected results. Companies are so hot to get on the technology bandwagon and make up for lost time in what the experts tout as the "PI space" that they buy the entire kit and caboodle. They buy learning management systems, employee performance support systems, online learning programs, outsourced learning resources, and anything else they can find that promises to get them the improvements they desire sooner.

Full-scale, rapid installment and organization-wide implementation are not for everybody. In fact, several reputable PI experts will join us in telling you that phased implementation is the best way to go. *Do a little bit at a time.* This way, you make sure each phase is working and creating its own return on investment before moving on to the next phase of PI.

With a full-scale, organization-wide implementation, it can take forever to get everyone on board with the corporate culture change. If performance improvement is also about change management, as many agree that it is, then it must follow the main principles for effective change management—namely, do it in stages to generate performers' acceptance of the new ways of performing and doing business.

MYTH 5: People will always adapt to and adopt the new PI technology.

TRUTH: It is people who will make the PI process work, so it is people who must learn how to use the new technology. This technology can be related to computers and software, as most people consider technology, or it can be related to the technology of performance improvement itself (theories, models, and interventions). Unfortunately, not everyone easily adapts to technology changes of any kind, while others do not readily adopt them.

You will need both a mind-set change and a corporate culture change before people will embrace the new PI technology or approach. This isn't to say people will sabotage the effort. More likely, they will do whatever they can to get by rather than fully embrace the new way to work. Before any company can expect a PI implementation to be successful, its leaders must make certain that all their people are on board with the effort. This again reinforces the importance of focusing on the people and not just the techniques in order to get positive performance improvement.

MYTH 6: PI is on the downswing due to high failure rates and the fact that most companies use only event-based training to improve performance.

TRUTH: PI is on the upswing, and it will become even more prevalent and relevant. Let's face it. PI is really nothing new. Parents, teachers, and coaches have been helping people improve their performance for hundreds of years. Now we have advanced technology and additional ways to make our jobs easier.

Nonetheless, no performance problem can be solved by event training. These one-off approaches to training may result in a slight performance improvement, but one that is rarely sustained over time. In fact, we firmly believe that any initial improvement is due to the Hawthorne effect. (This phenomenon was first described in a study many years ago at Western Electric's Hawthorne plant in Cicero, Illinois, where performance improved when the workers' environment was changed. For example, the lighting was changed and people did better. The truth, it later turned out, was that performance improved not because of the lighting but because management was now paying more attention to the employees.) When individual event trainings result in an immediate improvement in performance, the upswing is probably caused more by the change in attention (letting the employee go to the training) than by any other factor.

We believe that the high failure rates attributed to some PI implementations are due to three factors:

- Adopting a technology platform (EPSS, online learning, data collection and analysis), theory, or intervention before making certain the company has a strategic PI plan in place along with the appropriate processes and the people to implement PI

- Dropping the PI bomb (new measures, new expectations, new evaluation procedures) on employees instead of taking them through a culture change and preparing them for their new way to work

- Focusing on the internal workings of the new PI implementation from the corporate perspective instead of getting performers involved and creating a PI process that works with the way each performer wants to work with and for the company

MYTH 7: PI, as we know it today, is for everybody.

TRUTH: Although PI programs and approaches are available for companies of all sizes, high-level PI is not for everyone. You can't force square pegs into round holes. Many companies will survive and thrive very nicely by just focusing on hiring, recognizing (paying attention to), and keeping quality performers.

Now, we think that this is also PI, but in a different form. And if it is, then maybe it would be a good idea to look at how these non-high-tech companies are successfully implementing their PI approaches. Maybe the new approach to PI has to be one of first building relationships with the performers rather than managing their performances.

THE POSITIVE POWER OF FAILURE

Here is a bonus myth to work on: Failure is bad. Despite society's insistence that success is what is most important and failure is to be avoided, it's essential to revise that kind of thinking. Sometimes failure can result in positive performance improvement.

It seems such a dirty word to most people: *failure.* It creates so many negative images and fears that people quite often are afraid to try something for fear of failing. Yet unless you are willing to try something, anything, you'll never know how successful you could become.

Failure can be a positive force in your life. It all depends on how you look at it (perception) and what your attitude is about it. For example, do you know anyone who wanted to start a business or take a risk, yet listened to naysayers who maintained that the idea was destined to fail? Most of these negative people have never tried that particular thing themselves, but they are quick to give advice on why and how it is doomed to fail. Our advice is that when a lot of people tell you not to try something, and you really believe in it, you should go for it. More often than not, those people are projecting their fears onto you.

Here's another interesting thing about failure: People who are afraid to fail often go to the other extreme and try to be perfectionists. They are so hung up on doing everything perfectly that they never enjoy anything. And when they miss perfection, watch out! Do you know anyone like that? We're sure you do.

Another thing that scares people about failure is what others will think of them. You try something and you fail at it. What will your family and friends think? What will your co-workers and neighbors think? Really, who cares? You had an idea or a dream and you went for it. Congratulations! At least you won't be sitting around later in life wondering "what if."

Making Failure Work—To make failure work for you, embrace the attitude that with each mistake or failure, you can learn something and can improve for the next time. As we said before, failure is a function of perception and attitude.

Years ago, the story goes, a vice president walked into the office of Tom Watson Sr., the founder of IBM. The VP offered to resign because the huge project he'd been working on had blown up in his face and cost the *company $10 million. Watson said he would not fire the man or accept his resignation. When asked why, Watson replied that he had just spent $10 million educating the VP, so why would he fire him?*

How's that for a positive attitude toward failure? Take a lesson from Tom Watson and use failure as a learning experience. Failure is nothing more than feedback that something didn't work out quite right the first time. Learn from it and improve the next time.

You should also celebrate failure. Since you are going to learn a great deal from it, have a party. Make it something you embrace when it occurs. Celebrating failure will give you more confidence to try new things and not worry about mistakes.

Finally, stop being afraid of failure. It will not hurt you. Did you know that many millionaires and billionaires went bankrupt—some several times—before they made it? They failed in a big way before they succeeded. Thomas Edison failed at making the light bulb 10,000 times before he got it right. When he was asked why he persisted in the face of all those failures, he said he learned from each one how not to make a light bulb. Failure could have hurt him and scared him off. If it had, you might be reading this book by candlelight.

What Failure Really Means—Here is how we look at failure. We make it into an acronym that stands for the behaviors you should use whenever you make a mistake or fail. Learn this acronym and you'll welcome FAILURE and the positive power it brings to everything you do: *Feedback assures improved learning using revised expectations.*

Now, you may have heard of this approach to failure somewhere before. You may have read about it in another book or heard a speaker or trainer mention it during a program. We've been using it to help and motivate top performers for more than twenty-five years and we are sure that once you adopt this mind-set, you will see your own performance improve—as well as the performances of the people you manage.

Here are a few other things we know about top performers: They are more optimistic than pessimistic, especially in the face of failure. They tend to explain events and results in such a way that they are responsible for their results, yet negative outcomes are only temporary setbacks. They also feel they are in control of their lives more than do people who believe that mostly external forces have caused their failures. These positive top performers make their own luck, have more positive and healthier mental attitudes, and tend to deal with the stress of failure more effectively.

PRAISE FOR PERFORMANCE

Many companies today have returned to the concept of "pay for performance." This compensation approach requires the employee (performer) to be somewhat at risk with the company as compensation is based on outcomes. Many salespeople work this way, and it is very effective for them. However, other employees within a company are not used to working on commission, and they have difficulty achieving their performance goals when money is the primary reward. This results in lower financial compensation, decreased morale, and poorer productivity.

The reason pay for performance has regained popularity is that managers think employees are primarily motivated by money. Many recent surveys of managers and executives show them rating money as the main motivator for their employees. However, when the employees themselves are questioned, money is down in the middle or at the bottom of the list.

So what motivates employees more than money? If the answer is not pay for performance, what is the real answer to increasing employee motivation and improving performance?

Employees want PRAISE for performance. They want recognition and appreciation for a job well done, and they want to know that their work has meaning and impact.

We see "PRAISE" as an acronym for six behaviors or activities that managers can engage in that will motivate employees to perform at higher levels and achieve desired outcomes. The components are *praise, recognition, appreciation, inspiration, stroking,* and *encouragement.* Here is how to use them effectively to help elevate employee motivation and performance.

- **Praise:** In its simplest definition, praise involves saying positive things to people for what they've accomplished. The more lavish you are in your praise, the more you will help them raise their self-respect and self-esteem. Praise is a reinforcer, and—it's worth repeating—what gets reinforced gets repeated. So, if you want employees to do the right things well repeatedly, praise them for their efforts and accomplishments.

- **Recognition:** People love to be recognized for their accomplishments. Recognition comes in many forms, including verbal and written praise, awards and rewards, plaques, pins, T-shirts, public acknowledgment in front of co-workers, and a simple thank-you. In fact, when we ask groups if they hear the words *thank you* enough from their bosses, they all say no. Yet these same managers think they thank their employees often enough. Somewhere, there is a disconnect. If you want to start a very inexpensive and highly effective recognition program at your company, just make sure everyone starts to say "thank you" to everyone else. You'll be amazed at the results.

- **Appreciation:** As we said before, it has been well known in psychology for more than a hundred years that the thing people want most in life is to be appreciated by others, especially significant others. Employees want to be appreciated by their managers and their co-workers. Simple statements such as "I appreciate what you're doing" and "Your work is very much appreciated here" will create high levels of morale, increased intrinsic motivation to perform, and higher levels of performance. People who are appreciated know that their work has meaning and that they are making a difference. Every person wants to feel important and be made to feel important. Showing appreciation to someone does all this and more.

- **Inspiration:** Inspiration is the foundation of motivation and commitment. A major key to high-level performance is that the performer must be inspired to achieve. Creating an atmosphere of inclusion, empowerment, and consistent rewards for performance outcomes does this. Having the manager act as a role model for employees also does it. When managers walk the talk, they inspire others to do the same.

- **Stroking:** Everyone needs positive stroking. Strokes are what people give us for what we've done. They can be verbal, written, or graphic. Several of the simplest and most effective types of strokes are happy or smiley faces, JWD (Job Well Done) stickers, and "I like _____ because . . ." statements. You will be surprised at how much these three acknowledgments, in addition to other verbal strokes, can improve performance. Additionally, you may have some employees who need to be touched or physically stroked before they believe you are praising them. Do this appropriately, such as by patting them on the back or shoulder, in addition to these other stroking suggestions and you'll get the high levels of performance you desire.

- **Encouragement:** People want to believe in themselves and they want others to believe in them. Encouragement is a powerful leadership tool, especially when it comes from the heart. Let people know you expect the best from them and for them. Provide them with verbal, written, and physical feedback that will help them take their performance to the next level. Encourage them to do better, to be better, and to become better. They will exceed your expectations.

The results you'll achieve using this PRAISE for performance approach will definitely exceed the results from any pay for performance initiative. People want to be valued where they work and for what they do. PRAISE provides some of that value for them. It lets them know you care about them. It helps you tap into their hearts and minds, and it helps them tap into their inner drives and desires to be their best. If you have not yet implemented a PRAISE for performance approach, start one immediately. Establish your current performance baselines, begin your PRAISE for performance program, and see how much performance increases. If you've used pay for performance, compare the old with the new. You'll be pleasantly surprised at how well a simple behavior like praising someone can lead to powerful results and measurable performance improvement.

GOAL SETTING, EXPECTATIONS, AND REINFORCEMENT

Everyone talks about the importance of setting goals and using effective goal-setting techniques. Yet most people only pay lip service to goal setting. Even though they have been told to write down their goals and plan how to achieve them, they do not take the time or expend the effort to do so. Performers who don't write down goals and objectives and commit to them most likely will not achieve at the same level as those who do. And that is really too bad because goals and expectations for success help performers achieve great things. Expectations refer to a person's perceived probability of achieving success in relation to a goal. Since the manager and the performer should be working together to establish and align performance goals, they should also work together to set the performance expectations. Most of this responsibility, though, rests with the performer because only that person knows what he or she is truly capable of achieving. The manager must guide the performer in setting realistic goals and accurate expectations for success.

SMART GOAL SETTING

Most performers are familiar with the concept of SMART goal setting. This means that one's goals and objectives must be *specific, measurable, accomplishment based, realistic,* and *time based.* To translate that into a performance goal, you must specifically state what you want to accomplish, make sure the statement includes a measurement component, be certain you have the skills to achieve the realistic goal or objective, and ensure that you can accomplish it within a reasonable time frame. For example, a performance goal for a salesperson would be to increase sales by 10 percent during the next quarter as measured by gross revenues. A performance goal for a department could be exactly the same. The key is that you specify the measurable results, reinforcements, and consequences (what happens when people achieve or fall short of the goal) so that you can evaluate the end performance and make any changes that are necessary for future performances. SMART goal setting is, simply put, smart.

REINFORCING PERFORMANCE

There is a great deal to be said about the theory and science of reinforcement and how it affects ongoing and future performances. For our purposes, we want you to think about working with your performers to find out what reinforcements are most motivating to them. These can be things like a kind word, a show of appreciation, a plaque for recognition, paid time off, and even money. The key here is for the manager to work with the performer to identify appropriate reinforcements that are meaningful and relevant to the performer. Choosing reinforcements that you personally like without involving the performer may result in a decrease in future performances because the performer does not want the same types of reinforcements you do. So ask your people what will make them willingly repeat a successful performance.

THE MEASUREMENT AND EVALUATION SCOREBOARD

Think about sports for a minute. How many people would play (play, not practice) basketball, baseball, golf, tennis, soccer, or any other sport if no one kept score? How many people would compete without wanting to know how well they were doing compared to others and their own earlier efforts? Sometimes people keep score even in practice to measure their performance. Basketball players tell themselves they can't leave the court until they have made twenty foul shots in a row. Golfers make ten putts in a row before they leave the practice green. Tennis players get fifteen first serves in before they end their practice. Whatever the numbers are, it's human nature to keep score; we measure and evaluate our performances by the scoreboard.

The same is true in business. Human resources professionals are measured and evaluated by how many jobs they fill, how many employees they help the company retain, and how many successful succession plans they can help develop. Salespeople are measured and evaluated by the number of phone calls they make, the number of presentations or proposals they present, and of course, the number of sales they make. Managers are measured and evaluated by the number of employees they supervise, the productivity of their employees, and the contribution their employees make to the company's financial picture. In one way or another, everyone's performance is measured and evaluated.

The key is to make these measurements meaningful. This is why it is so important to establish quantifiable measures for all the goals you set. Just having a number attached to it does not make a goal meaningful to the individual or the company. There must be an alignment between what the person wants to achieve and what the company wants the person to achieve. If an employee regards $75,000 as an acceptable commission income level but the company has a target of $150,000, the two goals and the associated expectations are incompatible. The company will accomplish nothing by pursuing its goal except for the probable loss of that employee—who might well become a top producer if the goals can be brought into synch. So the key is to make sure that the individual goals align with the organizational goals and that the way the outcomes will be measured and evaluated is meaningful to both the performer and the company.

We have often been asked by clients how we determine what should be measured. The answer is really very simple. Find out what the performer wants to achieve, what the company wants and expects from the performer, and what it will cost to get the performer to that level. When the goals are aligned and the investment can pay for itself in a relatively short period, we can establish appropriate measurements. We like to use hard numbers because they are the true score. Whether they concern an income level, a rating scale, a dollar amount, pounds lost in a weight loss program, books read over a year, or something else, we prefer hard numbers. But it's not that we never pay attention to the soft numbers—the thoughts and feelings of the performers. We do want to know if people felt more or less anxiety while performing, if their stress levels decreased, if they felt better about performing under pressure, and how much improvement they believe they have made. These soft numbers are important to performance improvement and enhancement too. And if you feel you must have hard numbers for everything that matters, just ask the performer to rate his or her subjective states on some sort of scale. This will give you actual numbers you can work with as you evaluate the success of the performance and the effect the results have on the person and the organization.

RESULTS AND RETURNS

Do you remember how the big management fad in the 1990s was business process improvement and reengineering? Companies jumped on that bandwagon to standardize and systematize their processes in an effort to ensure quality. They worked hard to improve their processes, their throughput, and their process controls. The goal was to make everything work perfectly. And some companies actually succeeded. They developed better processes, received international certifications for the process work, and publicized how their improved processes led to greater productivity. Yet for all this process improvement, not everyone achieved positive results. You see, performance is like hitting a baseball. You have to keep your eye on the ball. In the case of process improvement, the batter (manager, employee, or organization) was too busy watching the pitcher's motion (the process) to remember to watch the ball. The goal is to hit the ball and achieve a result. If you don't keep your eye on the ball and swing the bat, you'll never hit it (get results). So our position is that process improvement does have a place, but it is not at the top of our list. To make sure you get the outcomes you want, help your people focus on the results of their performances and the returns the organization will receive for investing in them.

MORE THAN JUST FINANCIAL

You may be asking yourself what types of results you are looking for. These can be simple performance improvements such as retaining more employees, closing more sales, and increasing customer satisfaction. The desired results can also be decreases in errors, fewer repairs, and less rework. It doesn't really matter how the results are labeled as long as you can quantify and measure them. One of the reasons Positive CORE focuses on outcomes and results is that people do not perform in a vacuum. They want feedback and you can only give them feedback when you first specify the outcomes, determine the measurable results that are to be achieved, and then evaluate the performance in terms of those results. Positive feedback helps people improve their performances. Constructive feedback also helps them improve. The key is to link the feedback immediately to the results that are achieved. Then performers know how well they did according to the goals, expectations, and outcomes that were established.

As a manager, you invest in your employees. You put in time, energy, and effort, plus money in some cases—and you want to know that you're getting a reasonable return. So you do some calculations. Without going into high finance or complex math, you must know how much money you get back for how much you invest in a performer. For example, you approve a $500 expense for a training program for one employee. Following that training program, the employee increases production (performance) by a dollar value of $1,000. Your return on investment (ROI) in this case is 2:1. Obviously, the science of ROI is more complicated than this. It is sufficient to know that you've invested some sort of currency in your performers and you must know what you're getting back from them. By the way, you can calculate your ROI only if you know the results, not the processes. So keep your eye on the ball and get that hit.

Don't get caught in the trap of rewarding or reinforcing the performance effort instead of the outcome. You should reinforce both, but only when the effort leads to the desired outcome. Think back to what you read earlier in this chapter. If you want a behavior repeated, you reinforce it. If the behavior is appropriate, then you will get the performance results you desire over time. If the behavior is inappropriate, or is not getting the desired results, why would you reinforce it? Simply reinforcing the effort of a performer may motivate that performer to continue to exert effort, but it won't get you any closer to improved performance. You must reinforce the efforts that approximate the desired performance because you are measuring the success of that performer based on the results produced. Rewarding effort is a motivator, but nonetheless, any effort leading to a poor performance should not be reinforced. In the long run, you won't be happy and neither will the performer. So reward effort only when it leads to the desired results.

POSITIVE CORE PLUS PERSONAL AND SOCIETAL BENEFITS

It is one thing to do everything you can to better yourself: read, take training classes, go for coaching and counseling, practice your skills, and generally try to be the best you can be. It is quite another to consider how everything you do affects not only your life but also the lives of others. By focusing on your strengths and the positives you bring to a situation, you can ultimately create improvement across the board. Since one of the principles of positive psychology is to make this a healthier and better world, you must consider how the Positive CORE approach achieves this goal.

Very few people consider the effects their individual performance may have on society. Hardly anyone takes an idealistic or a holistic view of how that one butterfly flapping its wings in China can cause a tornado in Kansas. Even fewer people consider how what they do today affects the grandchildren and great-grandchildren they have or may one day have. Positive CORE promotes the long-term positive view of how today's performances affect tomorrow's performers. Here are a few outcomes, both qualitative and quantitative, you should consider from a Positive CORE perspective:

- All people play to their strengths and love who they are.
- All people love what they do and do what they love.
- Poverty, famine, and disease no longer exist.
- People and companies work for the greater good of society.
- Relationships between people, among organizations, and across nations improve.
- All people receive a quality education in school, and adults continue to educate themselves both on and off the job.
- Our children and grandchildren may have it easier than we do but not so easy that they do not learn to do for themselves.
- Crime diminishes or maybe even disappears.
- All people know what is expected of them in all situations in all places all the time.
- Performances are measurably improved, and productivity measurably increases, which means more is being done in less time with less stress.

These are just a few of the outcomes we can consider through the Positive CORE model. A quantitative and quantifiable metric can be put on each of those desired results so that people can measure progress and success in achieving them—and provide appropriate feedback to performers to help them continue to improve and enhance their performances. The end result is that ordinary performers become extraordinary performers, others go from good to great, and we all create an organization (and a world) of top performers.

OUR CHALLENGE TO YOU

Think about the outcomes you are trying to achieve in your company, or within your own job. What will you do differently now when you consider the points made in this chapter? How will you establish employee recognition programs? What do you personally require in the way of positive reinforcement, and how will you provide the same for your employees? Take a look at your company compensation and reward programs. What can you do to make them more meaningful and relevant to your employees? How can you improve these programs?

Also, review how you measure performance. If you are expecting certain outcomes and accomplishments from your people, yet you do not have a scoreboard for them to see how they are doing, you will have disconnects. These disconnects will be in expectations and interpretations related to the desired performance as well as in the evaluation of the performance efforts. You may find that you believe one thing should have been done and your employee believes another thing was expected. The disconnect will hold both of you back if you do not clearly communicate with each other. So challenge yourself to establish measurable outcomes of everyone's performance, develop positive reinforcement programs that are meaningful and motivating to each individual performer, and always consider the bigger picture of the impact of everyone's performance on the organization, the community, and society.

— S I X —

RELATIONSHIPS

TLC in the Workplace

Take a moment to think about your relationships. Which of them are good and which need work? What makes the good ones good and the poor ones bad? If you've ever been in a serious relationship, why did you fall in love with that person? Why did you marry that person, if you did? Also, think back to some of your previous jobs, or even your current job. Who do you get along with on the job, and why? Which of your employees do you like to work with and which ones do you try to avoid? What are the reasons for these relationships, and how do these relationships affect the overall performance of everyone involved?

These are important questions. Good interpersonal relationships are among the main keys to success in any organization. Books on emotional intelligence, moral intelligence, happy home lives, and leadership all talk about the importance of getting along well with people. There may be

TABLE 6: POSITIVE CORE ELEMENTS			
Confidence	*Outcomes*	*Relationships*	*Engagement*
Self-esteem	Goals, expectations, and reinforcements	Managers	Commitment
Strengths and talents	Measurement and evaluation	Friends and family	Emotions
Reinforcements and consequences	Results and returns: individuals, organizations, and society	Social, professional, and community contacts	Motivation and optimism

some situations where leaders are able to coerce followers into performing in the absence of a good relationship, but most people need a positive relationship with their boss if they are to overachieve and exceed expectations. The same is true in your family. Partners and children will reach higher performance levels in everything they do when they feel comfortable and secure in their relationships at home. Students in school who like their teachers and feel comfortable with them (that is, have a good relationship with them) usually outperform their counterparts on tests.

Even though much of the literature linking relationships to performance is anecdotal, it's easy to see that building and maintaining strong relationships among people who interact every day is vital to success. In fact, research completed by the Gallup organization and several other private companies and professional associations concludes that the main reason people stay with or leave a company is their relationship with their supervisor. As we've said elsewhere in this book, it's not necessarily the money and prestige that motivate someone to do a good job. More often than not, it is the personal relationships and emotional support that help people be successful and keep them happy.

A couple of years ago, we were asked to coach a senior executive in a large corporation. This person had all the tools to be successful but, for some reason, was not achieving his personal goals. His group was also not achieving their goals. As we interviewed the executive, we learned that he had certain beliefs about how the job should be done. First, he was the boss—so his way was the right way. He did not need or request input from his direct reports; he just expected them to do what he said. Second, he was totally responsible for all the success that occurred but had no part in anything that fell short of achieving the goal. He laid that on his people. And third, he did not see anything wrong with his relationships at work.

As you can imagine, breaking through these perceptual and behavioral barriers was no easy task. Yet, over time, we were able to help this executive see that his success was directly dependent on the success of his people. We taught him to listen attentively to the people in his department and to thank them for their input. We gave him tasks to perform to change his behavior so he would show his people that he truly cared about them. Of course, his staff met these first attempts with skepticism. Over time, though, as his behavior remained consistent, his team turned around. Since he was asking for their input and trusting them more, they began to trust him more. Since he began to share credit for success and responsibility *for failure, his team became more trusting of him. And as soon as he was comfortable with letting his people do their thing (play to their strengths), the performance of his department skyrocketed. All this was a result of improving his relationships with his people.*

SEVEN BUILDING BLOCKS OF GREAT RELATIONSHIPS

Our work with individuals and organizations has enabled us to learn a great deal about what makes a great relationship, and what it takes to build one. Our marriage of over twenty-five years has also helped us learn what it takes to develop and strengthen the foundations of relationships, and we've been able to take these elements and devise an easy-to-remember acronym for building great relationships. The seven building blocks of great relationships form the word RESPECT. Here is how RESPECT— spelled out by *rapport, empathy, service, passion, expectations, commitment,* and *trust*—helps you build great relationships.

RAPPORT

Rapport is the ability to align yourself with someone and to get along with that person. It is the ability to connect with that person so that you develop mutual trust and understanding. Since trust is another of the seven building blocks, you can see the importance of developing rapport first. You won't have a relationship if you cannot establish rapport.

A number of techniques can help you build rapport with someone else. You can talk about shared likes and dislikes. You can match your breathing rate, speaking rate, and body posture to those of the person you're talking with. You can use similar words, language patterns, and jargon. You can also agree with the other person's political and life views. In any case, you must make a connection to establish rapport. Remember that people like people who are like them. They gravitate toward people who share similar ideas, philosophies, principles, values, and beliefs. It's human nature: we are most comfortable with people who are most like us. And people who are most like us usually like us the most. That is what rapport is all about.

Take a look at several relationships, some that you think are good and some that are shaky. What is the connection between the people in these relationships? How well are they aligned? How aware are they of each other's thoughts and feelings, and what do they do to make each other comfortable? In the relationships that you think are shaky, what is the disconnect? How are the people misaligned? Figure out these answers and you're well on your way to understanding the basic principles of building and maintaining rapport.

EMPATHY

Empathy is the ability to understand how someone else feels. It does not mean you have to know exactly how someone feels about something, nor is it sympathy, where you feel sorry for someone or his or her situation. Empathy is all about genuine understanding. It's the ability to take off your shoes before you walk a mile in someone else's shoes. It's the ability to support someone who is basking in the glory of success or grieving because of a loss. Empathy is the feeling you have for someone, about someone, or with someone without grabbing the spotlight or truly sharing the pain. Empathy is communicating to the other person that you are there for support, in good times and bad, and that you understand what he or she is going through.

Higher levels of empathy will also lead to compassion and forgiveness. These are two emotional competencies that are required to maintain a long-term relationship. When you know and understand how someone feels, and you can be compassionate about it, you solidify your relationship with that person. If someone has done something to hurt you, and you understand what was done and why, and you can still forgive the person, you will be solidifying your relationship. Like all the other building blocks of a great relationship, empathy has its offshoots.

SERVICE

A great many publications focus on the importance of being a servant leader—putting your people first and helping them succeed. There are just as many publications on the importance of customer service, or service to customers. In any relationship, service to the other person is critical. What you do to help that person, how you help that person, and when you help that person all make up the service component of building great relationships.

Part of providing service to another person is being available when he or she needs you. If you're around only when you need that person or need something from him or her, your relationship is doomed. Without reciprocity, the other party eventually will leave because of your selfishness. However, when you give first, and give before you get, your returns will be greatly magnified. Helping other people get what they want in life first (service to others) will get you more of what you want. And, in business, it will help you and your team achieve great things.

In recent years, there has been a push in business away from the concept that the customer comes first. The move is toward putting the *employee* first and letting the customer come second. High-performing organizations take care of their people first so their people can take care of their customers. Consider this approach and its effect and transfer it to your relationships with your people.

PASSION

You might think it is crazy to talk about passion in a book that tells you how to get the best performance out of the people in your company. Yet passion is a critical element in driving performance and building relationships. You can call it what you will: passion, desire, enthusiasm. Some may even call it love. As a matter of fact, a few years ago, we told a group of CEOs that they had to love their employees. They had to show passion in how they felt about them. Now, we clarified we were not talking about romantic love. We were talking about showing people that you care about them. The CEOs who took this in a positive light went on to grow their companies, while the ones who did not see the relationship between passion and performance continued to lead stagnant companies.

We also talk about passion as it relates to managers in another way. In addition to being passionate about your people, you must also be passionate about the work you do. People will want to work for you if they see that you are truly in love with what you do. People want to be around passionate people. Passionate managers and leaders have a built-in charisma factor that works as a magnet to attract top performers. It enables everyone to get along better because you are all on the same high-level page. If we were to give you one piece of advice about passion, it would be not only to love what you do and the people you do it with but to show that love. Make your passion for your job and your people visible. Let everyone know how you feel as you care for and support your people and the job they are all doing. Your performance results will be beyond expectations.

EXPECTATIONS

This building block has probably derailed more relationships than any other. What you expect of people in a relationship must be clearly communicated. You cannot leave anything to chance. If you expect someone to do something a certain way or complete a task at a certain time, you must say so and make sure the person understands. If you expect performance to reach a certain level, you must clearly communicate that also. Failure to do so can irreparably damage a relationship.

How many times when something goes wrong between two people have you heard one of them say, "I thought you knew what I wanted you to do," or something to that effect? Your people are not mind readers. You should not expect anyone to figure out what you are thinking or what you mean by what you say or don't say. If you have an expectation of people, make sure they totally understand what you want them to do, how you will measure their success, and how they will know if they have met your expectations.

This is so important to performance and relationship success that an entire branch of motivational psychology has grown up around what is called *expectancy theory*. Basically, expectancy theory says that you will perform in accordance with your expectations of success or with how important achievement of this task is to you. Translate this to your relationships. You will put effort into a relationship based on how much you expect to get out of it, how much you can contribute to the success of it, or how important maintaining that relationship is to you.

Look at your successful business relationships. We will bet that the most successful of them are those in which you know what is expected of you by the other person and the other person knows what you expect of him or her. Your poor relationships are probably missing this factor. The same is true in your personal relationships. Those that you have built into positive relationships will have clearly communicated expectations. Those that are teetering on the brink of collapse will have either unclear expectations or no expectations at all. The bottom line is to establish your expectations and clearly communicate them to help you build strong relationships.

COMMITMENT

Commitment is closely related to passion as well as to engagement (see Chapter 7). For a relationship to sustain itself, each participant must be committed to the other person. Just as you are committed to your job, you must be equally committed to the people in your relationships.

Commitment is as much emotional as it is behavioral. You must commit yourself in your mind before you show commitment through your behaviors. Commitment will be evidenced by how you feel about someone, what you say to and about someone, how comfortable you are around that person (rapport also), and how much you want to help that person succeed. Commitment is not a sometime thing or a partial thing. When you are in a relationship, you are either totally committed or you are not committed. Successful relationships cannot be built on partial commitments. When people try to be partially or sometimes committed to a relationship, that relationship suffers. Evidence of a lack of commitment, and it does not matter if it's a business or personal relationship, includes cheating, lying, stealing, one-upmanship, and a variety of other negative behaviors and activities. So to have a successful relationship, you must commit to being totally involved in that relationship.

TRUST

Trust is the cornerstone of any relationship. While rapport gets a relationship started and helps keep it going over time, trust is the glue that holds it together. A person who is trustworthy creates trust in a relationship. A successful relationship ensures that trust is a two-way street. It's possible for one person to trust another more than the second person trusts the first, but the relationship will not succeed over time because the trust is not mutually reciprocated. Trust must be given and received if the relationship is to work effectively.

Trustworthiness is a function of character and competence (overt behavior). A person who is trustworthy is someone who establishes and lives by a set of positive principles, values, and beliefs and does not let anything minimize that trio. Living this way makes people trustworthy; you can trust that they will do what they say, they will act in a predictable way in a given situation, and they will do everything possible to maintain their trustworthiness. That is the competence, or behavioral, part of trust. You behave in ways that exhibit trust. A person you can trust is willing to trust you as well until you do something that betrays that trust. This is true in all healthy relationships, both personal and professional.

In a high-trust relationship, the parties tolerate each other's strengths and weaknesses. They tend to be understanding if one makes a mistake or lets the other down for some reason. Communication is faster and more effective when people trust each other. That's because they believe each other and believe in each other. They know neither will do anything to deliberately hurt the other. They know they both value the relationship. They both work hard to reciprocate an understanding of the other person before trying to get a point across. People listen more attentively when they trust someone because they know the trusted party has their best interests at heart. And trustworthy people respond accordingly.

Here are a few things you can do to build trust in a relationship. Be trustworthy. When you make a promise, keep it. Do what you say you're going to do when you say you're going to do it. This builds your credibility and ties trust to commitment, which cements these two building blocks even more. When you are honest and trustworthy, people assign the value of integrity to you and they know they can count on you. You can also build trust through what are sometimes called "random acts of kindness." When you do things for people just for the sake of doing them, and you do this over time, people come to trust you as someone who has no ulterior motives. Their trust level for you keeps growing and growing. In business, high levels of trust also help you help your performers do a better job. That's because they will be more receptive to your feedback. They know that you are being honest with them and giving them this feedback only to help them, not to hurt them. They will reciprocate by trusting you even more and doing a better job for themselves and for you.

And isn't all that the purpose of a manager and a leader—to get things done through people? High-performing people and organizations realize the value of having a team of people with them and behind them. The relationships among these team (or group or department) members are critical to ongoing success. The relationships form the core of the efforts for successful performance.

Once you've formed trusting relationships, you have to maintain and sustain them. You do this by doing the following:

- **Taking your time:** Relationships don't get built overnight and they don't get stronger by waving a magic wand. Take the time to build rapport, trust, and credibility and to strengthen your relationships.

- **Listening attentively:** More relationships are destroyed because people do not listen to each other than because of any overt action. Let other people speak first and work hard to understand their point of view before trying to get them to understand yours.

- **Recognizing and appreciating people:** The number one human need is to feel appreciated. Let people know you appreciate their efforts and you care about them. Tell them, show them, and do things for them. Your returns will be enormous.

- **Seeking common ground:** Sometimes even the best relationships hit a roadblock or a bump in the road. When this happens, go back to your rapport building and seek common ground. Find out where you agree, go for a win-win, and work together to repair any damage.

Since the relationship has been positive and strong up to this point, you'll find that you have many more positives than negatives. Focus on the positives.

- **Doing the unexpected:** Most people love positive surprises. Take some action that results in a pleasant surprise for the other person in this relationship. If it is one of your employees, provide a day off, or tickets to a movie, or something else the person wants. Offer a special or high-visibility project with a real chance to make a mark. Be different and allow your people to be different. You'll find that doing the unexpected in a positive manner spices up the relationship and leads to better performance.

Focus on these building blocks and you'll have a strong foundation for your Positive CORE, which will lead to high performance.

FRIENDS ON THE JOB

It is basically good old common sense that performance on the job is directly affected by the kind of relationship people have with their managers. The comfort of a positive relationship or the tension and anxiety of a negative relationship will definitely affect how well they do their jobs. In fact, we can almost say that the manager has a greater impact on a team member's performance than any other factor, assuming that the person has the skills and resources to do the job.

Think about it. How many people do you know who did not like their managers? How many of those people went out of their way to do their jobs just well enough to not get fired? And how many others did what they could to make themselves look good and their managers look bad? The unfortunate answer is that most people who do not like or get along well with their managers underperform. Whether they do this on purpose or simply because they lack the motivation to do the job well is only slightly relevant here. The important point is that managers affect how well people do.

The performance and productivity of your employees are a direct reflection of their relationship with you. As we've said, research by several organizations has shown that people either stayed with a company or left it for another job simply because they liked or disliked their manager and supervisor. The Society for Human Resource Management (SHRM) says that 80 percent of employees leave their jobs because they don't feel appreciated or recognized by their managers. So it's not about salary, incentives, or benefits. It's a relationship thing. Employees will go through brick walls for their managers if there is a good relationship there.

One financial services company had a department manager who really got on the nerves of senior management. He was gruff, spoke out of turn at department head meetings, and just seemed to have a rough manner that did not fit in with this conservative organization. Word got around that he was going to be fired. When his team found out about this, they all but rebelled. Senior management could not understand why people would rally around him so strongly since he had all these negative behaviors and characteristics. So somebody in the C-suite got smart and started to watch the department head as he worked with his team. What this executive learned was that the manager was always there at the close of business thanking his team for coming to work that day and for the effort they put in. He told them how much he appreciated them and that he was grateful to have them on his team. That was it. That was all he did. And it was more than enough. The executive team wound up deciding not only to keep this manager but to have other managers follow his example with their team members.

Remember what we said about praise and its power earlier in the book. Here you get a chance to see how it works with regard to developing powerful and positive relationships between managers and employees.

ORGANIZATIONAL RELATIONSHIPS

Organizations that perform well have positive relationships throughout. These relationships are based on mutual understanding, trust, respect, and a cooperative spirit to achieve the individual and organizational goals. When these values exist and are evident through general behavior patterns, performance is enhanced. When these values are absent, performance declines. In fact, in an organizational atmosphere that lacks these values and undervalues appreciation of its employees, performance will always be below potential. Just look at the recent collapses of some of the major companies in the United States. Enron, Arthur Andersen, WorldCom, and several others did not have good relationships among all their team members. While the senior management team may have had good relationships among its members, they certainly did not care about the rest of the people. So these once-high-flying companies crashed and burned. On the other hand, companies like Raymond James and Associates (financial services), SAS (computer software), Lexus of Tampa Bay, and Ritz Carlton Hotels promote positive relationships between their managers and employees. It is these companies, and those like them, that thrive in every kind of economy.

RELATIONSHIPS BETWEEN MANAGERS AND TEAM MEMBERS

We have had the pleasure of working with several companies that maintain positive relationships, and we were fascinated by the loyalty, motivation, and commitment of their employees. They loved their managers and said they would not want to work for anyone else. They said they stayed in their current positions because of their relationships with their managers, even though at times they had been offered more money to change jobs. They said their managers made them feel important, appreciated, and valued. They also said their managers told them that the work they were doing made a difference in people's lives. How can you not want to work with and for someone who values you, appreciates what you accomplish, and sees the impact of your work on others? It is these critical elements that make the relationship between manager and employees among the most important in any organization.

All organizations have a variety of relationship structures that affect how things get done. There are reporting relationships, working relationships, quality-check relationships, and, of course, romantic relationships (but we won't get into that last one here). Think about the relationship structures in your organization. How well are they designed? Do they enhance or hinder communication, customer service, or productivity? Do the people in your organization know who they are related to and how this affects their work? Or are their relationships mixed up, messed up, and confusing? If the relationship with you, the manager, is so important to the successful performance of a team member and the overall success of the organization, what are you doing about making sure all your relationships are positive?

RELATIONSHIPS BETWEEN EMPLOYEES

One other type of relationship is right up there with the relationship between manager and team members. That is the relationship between employees. Everyone wants a best friend on the job—a fellow worker to talk to, trust, and maybe even socialize with. As a manager, you're best off if you do everything in your power to make it easy for your employees to make friends with each other. Now, you've probably heard many times that people don't have to be best friends on the job; they just have to be able to work together. That may have been true in the past, but today, high performance and positive performance improvement both depend on people having someone else they can count on, trust to be there for them, and make their life a little bit easier on the job. Think back to any time in your work career when you really enjoyed what you were doing. It could even be right now. Who were the people you enjoyed spending time with at work? How much did these people motivate you, make you laugh, help lift you up if you were down, and teach you new ways to do your job better? These were your best friends on the job, and they made your life richer and more fulfilling. They made it easy for you to come to work. So, as a manager, part of your job is to make sure your team members develop and cultivate on-the-job friendships.

BUILDING POSITIVE RELATIONSHIPS WITH FRIENDS, FAMILY, AND CO-WORKERS

People who are married live longer than people who are single or divorced. People who have healthy social networks are happier than people who are loners. And people with a happy family life lead happier lives overall.

OK, so maybe we don't have scientific data to back up those statements. Most people would agree, though, that they make sense. Human nature again: we are happier when we have friends and are doing things we enjoy. We are happier when our family members are getting along, with no stress or tension in the relationships. And we are all certainly happier when our relationship with our significant other is working. We know these things to be true even if no one can cite an original research study on the subject.

So, if that's the case, why don't more organizations encourage the development of relationships with friends and families? Workplaces that have day care centers get better productivity out of the parents whose children are taken care of on-site. Parents take fewer sick days because of their children. This, too, serves to enhance performance and increase productivity. One hospital not only developed a day care center for its employees but added a "sick care" center, where parents could bring children who had colds or coughs. And the center was staffed by nurses. Perhaps even more important, the hospital eventually opened these centers up to the community to help out parents, even those who did not work at the hospital. The reasoning was that if more people were able to work without worrying about who was taking care of their children, then the performance and productivity of the entire community would increase. The hospital was right. More people were working without stress, tension, and anxiety—and doing a better job. The relationship between the hospital and the community continued to grow, and people had nothing but positive things to say about the service the hospital was providing.

Other area companies followed the hospital's lead. They reasoned that if family relationships were well founded and well grounded, then employees would bring more energy and motivation to work. Companies began hosting family events, inviting family members to the job, and making a big deal about bring-your-child-to-work day. Imagine the positive energy that coursed through this community's veins as everyone was performing at peak levels because relationships between individuals and organizations were extremely positive and mutually beneficial. And imagine the offshoots of this as people began to form friendships with other parents at the centers, at the events, and even in their own companies. Positive performance enhancement became the norm rather than a hoped-for achievement.

There is another reason for you, as a manager, to promote positive relationships on the job. You can always use "bench strength"—people able to step right in and do the job when you require someone to do so. You also want to make sure your succession plans are in place, which means always being on the lookout to hire top people. Now, you can spend a great deal of money on ads to recruit new hires. You can spend money on job fairs and trade shows. Or you can go to the best source of new hires and positive performers: your own people. Think about how powerful your team would be if your employees were able to work with their friends—people they like and who are like them. The atmosphere would be electric. The pace would be positively maddening. And the results would be fantastic.

Take a moment to imagine it. Friends who really get along are working next to their best friends. Everyone is helping everyone else. Performance and productivity are at all-time highs. You let your people bring their family members to work. You help them strengthen those family relationships because now their spouses and children better understand what they do. With that comes more freedom and less worry. Motivated, happy employees are performing at their highest possible levels because they like their jobs and the people they work with. The result is better performance all around.

THE SOCIAL NETWORK PROCESS MAP

Here's something you should try with your team members. It comes from social psychology and sociology and it will give you a good visual on who likes whom and how the relationships in your organization play out.

- Ask your team members to write down the names of three of their co-workers they like the best as people, and then three names of those they like working with the best. These names can be the same but it is not necessary.

- When you have collected all the names on both lists, write down how many times each person is named and by whom. You can eventually draw a series of circles with everyone's name in an individual circle.

- Draw connector lines from each person's name to all the people that person listed. (You're interested in how many people get named by others, but the lines are easier to draw in this direction.)

- When you have completed this circle chart, take a look at who has the most connector lines. This person is called your "star" or central social figure. If it is the same person from the lists for both "like most" and "like to work with most," then you definitely must find out how this person operates and why everyone reacts so favorably.

When you learn the desirable behaviors and strategies, work hard to have everyone model them so your organization's social network will strengthen. If you have outliers, or people with no incoming connector lines, you'll need to find out why this is so and work to remedy the situation. Remember, your team requires a strong social network (friends and friends who feel like family on the job) to perform at its best. It is true that a few people prefer to be alone and are still top performers. If you find you have any of this rare breed, allow them their liberties. In most cases, though, people draw energy from being around others, so it might as well be positive energy. Chart and draw your team's social networks and see how you can develop positive performance improvements by strengthening the network.

SIX DEGREES OF KEVIN BACON

You're probably wondering what Kevin Bacon is doing in that head. You were probably expecting something like "six degrees of separation." Most people have heard about the theory that everyone on the planet is separated by only six contacts from anyone else on the planet. This concept, which grew out of a social psychology experiment decades ago, says that through knowing someone who knows someone who knows someone, and so on, you can get in touch with anyone you want to reach anywhere in the world. The six degrees of separation grew into a parlor game called "Six Degrees of Kevin Bacon," in which people attempted to show how the actor Kevin Bacon was connected to anyone and everyone in Hollywood and the world. For example, say that one wanted to find out how many steps it took to connect Bacon to Debbie Allen, the choreographer and actress. Bacon was in a movie with Lori Singer, who played a student on the TV show *Fame,* which also starred Debbie Allen. So Bacon was only two degrees of separation from Allen. That's how the parlor game was played. The concept also serves as the basis for several social networking Web sites, such as www.friendster.com, www.linkedin.com, and www.myspace.com.

The purpose of such social networking Web sites, networking groups, and even corporate sports teams is to promote socialization, connectedness, and the building of relationships, which can be accomplished through continuous and consistent contact, by finding common ground, and by developing rapport and trust. The power of relationships, as mentioned earlier in this chapter, also extends to mental and physical health, quality of life, and the ability to perform at high levels.

Remember that top performers in any organization say they work well when they like and trust their manager; they have someone they consider a "best friend" at work; and they are reinforced for the outcomes of their behaviors by co-workers, their manager, or senior management. This is all based on the quality of the relationships.

BEING PART OF SOMETHING

Years ago, employees were told to leave their personal lives at the door when they came to work. Today's wisdom is that it is the total person who comes to work every day. Team members bring their hopes and fears, their emotions and knowledge, and their motivation in with them. You can't expect them to arrive and thrive in isolation. Humans are social animals, meant to be part of something. It is in our DNA. Even our prehistoric ancestors realized the value of building relationships. The more people that banded together, the greater their chances for survival. Some would hunt, while others protected the newly formed tribe from animals and other tribes. People banded together to keep warm, to care for each other when they got sick, and to help each other improve in multiple ways. The desire to be part of a group is hardwired into all of us.

Consider this. Have you ever gone out with your spouse or significant other and, after an hour or two, you run out of things to talk about? As you sit there wondering what to say or do next, another couple you're friends with comes by and you gladly invite them to join your twosome. All of a sudden, the conversation picks up, everyone gets more animated, and there are plenty of things to talk about—even with your spouse. Or take this example. You're in a room with a very small group of people. As more and more people enter the group, the buzz picks up and gets louder. While some of the loudness is due to more people talking, much of it is due to the energy these people are creating by being together. In your role as a manager, do you generate energy with and for your people, or do you stifle it? Do you encourage group interaction, or do you keep people from each other so you can maintain control? High performance comes with growing energy and interaction.

SOCIAL GROUPS

Encourage your team members to form social groups or networks. These can be on the job and in their personal lives. Give them outlets at work to meet, greet, and converse with each other.

You should also give them outlets to blow off some steam. Think about getting your people involved in recreational sports leagues, corporate athletic programs, or volunteering in the community.

Many companies that provide social outlets for their people see performance and productivity increase because the team members intrinsically want to give back to the organization because the organization is doing something for them. Imagine the atmosphere, feelings, and thoughts of this company. Now contrast those with the same things in a company that does nothing to foster relationships. This second company is always looking to catch its people doing something wrong instead of something right. Which company would you like to work in? We know it's not the second company. So which company do you think your people would like to work in? Since your people are just like you, do what you can to create the atmosphere of the first company. You'll be rewarded many times over with higher performance.

ASSOCIATIONS

Another way to build social ties is to encourage your people to participate in professional associations and networking meetings. Have them get out and meet other people like themselves, and encourage them to get others involved. Remember that the building of relationships and the socialization that comes with it have a positive effect on employees' performance on the job. As to the question of who will pay for these memberships, if your organization can afford it, the company should pay for at least one or two professional association memberships for each of your team members. This is very similar to the concept of tuition reimbursement. If your people want to continue their education and your company is willing to pay for their schooling, why wouldn't it pay for their social schooling in the real world? You can always establish a policy on memberships and how many you will pay for. When you do pay for them, your people will repay you many times over with improved performance. If nothing else, the psychological law of reciprocity, whereby they feel they must do something positive for you or the organization because you did something positive for them, will come into play here. Meanwhile, your people will start to feel better about themselves because they are involved with other people, and this will translate into better performance.

COMMUNITY ACTIVITIES

You can also help people take their social ties to another playing field. Work with your team to get involved in the community. This can involve working with children, seniors, charities, or any number of community organizations. One company we worked with gave its employees paid time off to be tutors and mentors to elementary school pupils in a disadvantaged neighborhood. The results of this effort included improved grades for the students, ongoing positive publicity for the company, and an increase in performance for the employees. In fact, the improved performance led to increased value for the company, and this once small, privately owned company was bought out by a major corporation for tens of millions of dollars. Impressive as that is, what was even more impressive to us was that the new parent company realized the value of community involvement and allowed the employees to continue to serve. Year after year, the parent company benefited from an ongoing increase in productivity. Was the workforce any smarter or was the technology any better? Possibly. But during our interviews, we learned that the people felt it was their ability to socialize on and off the job that kept them highly motivated to perform at higher and higher levels. They were more engaged in their work (a topic we revisit in Chapter 7).

Think about what you do outside work and your relationships there. Do you play in a recreational sports league, or do you coach a youth sports team? Do you donate time to your church or synagogue or to a charity? Do you mentor children at a school or drop in to visit an elderly person who has no other family? What is it that you do to build and develop other relationships, and how does what you do make you feel? We're sure you feel very good about what you do and it motivates you to want to do even better the next time.

So what does all this touchy-feely stuff have to do with organizational performance and effectiveness? How can we quantify the effect of relationships on improved performance when relationships cannot be measured? The answer is simple. Things that contribute to relationships can be measured. The various types of motivation can be measured, and motivation affects performance outcomes. The various types of intelligence (emotional, moral, social, practical) can be measured, and they affect the quality of relationships. And personality or behavioral types can be measured and determined, and they will help you connect the people who will feel most comfortable together in a relationship.

Relationships are powerful contributors to performance, and especially to performance improvement. Build positive relationships with your people, and you will see their performances soar, as will yours. Coming to work will be fun, not drudgery. Doing the job right the first time will be the norm, and previously high levels of performance will become the baseline. You'll be able to objectively measure output and outcomes based on the quality of the relationships you develop with your people and those they develop with each other.

OUR CHALLENGE TO YOU

Actually, we believe so strongly in this part of the CORE model that we have a few challenges for you. The first is to map out all your relationships with your people. Use a simple rating scale of 1 to 10, with 10 being the best, and rate your relationship quality with each person. Then, match that rating to the person's performance levels.

Next, identify your top two or three performers. Unless their jobs require them to work alone or in isolation, you will probably find that they have several strong relationships with people at work. If you ask them, they will almost certainly tell you that they have strong relationships with people outside work. Go to another level and find out if these star performers with the more positive relationships are also happier on the job. You may find a direct link between relationships, success, and happiness. And if (not really if, but when) you do, you'll find that relationship building is critical to your own success and the success of your organization.

One other thing you should do: Think back to the social network process map we had you develop earlier in the chapter to identify your social stars. Review that to see the links between people. See if your social stars on the map are your star performers on the job. Find out why people like to be around these social stars. In most cases, you will find a positive relationship between high performance and likeable people. This really makes our final challenge to you very easy.

Figure out what you are going to do to build strong relationships with your team members, to make sure they have at least one best friend at work, and to get them involved with other people and organizations. When you build up this relationship capital, it will easily translate into financial capital, and the social benefits that will grow from this will also be very positive.

— *S E V E N* —

ENGAGEMENT

The Foundation for Effort and Execution

E ngagement is a hot topic today. People talk about having employees who are fully engaged. Companies want to engage their employees in order to retain them. Athletic teams get their players engaged in the program so they buy into the system, the hard practices, and the goals of the team. Ongoing research is being conducted that reveals engaged performers are better performers, happier performers, and more motivated performers. While the PI field used to talk about motivating people to perform well, now it seems that just being motivated is not enough. You have to be fully engaged.

What does being engaged in a performance really mean? It means that you are committed to your actions and the desired and expected outcomes. It also means that you have high levels of intrinsic motivation,

TABLE 7: POSITIVE CORE ELEMENTS			
Confidence	*Outcomes*	*Relationships*	*Engagement*
Self-esteem	Goals, expecta-tions, and rein-forcements	Managers	Commitment
Strengths and talents	Measurement and evaluation	Friends and family	Emotions
Reinforcements and consequences	Results and returns: individuals, organizations, and society	Social, professional, and community contacts	Motivation and optimism

which come from developing realistic expectations about your performance and having an optimistic attitude about what you can achieve. You are also aware of and in control of your emotions—you have what's currently called *emotional intelligence.* And along these same lines, being engaged means that you seek out stress because it pumps you up. You know that your performance may fluctuate from time to time so you have to be resilient to combat the effects of stress, to get up when you get knocked down, and to thrive in each and every performance situation. When you combine your high levels of commitment, optimism, and intrinsic motivation with the control of your emotions in a task that is both challenging and rewarding, you become fully engaged and enter the psychological state of flow.

In Chapter 1, we talked about the the importance of attending more to the psychology of the people involved than to the processes and models of performance improvement, emphasizing the importance of taking this softer, more positive approach instead of the typical mechanistic approach to performance improvement. In this chapter, we expand that focus so you become aware of the needs, desires, and motivations of your performers. With that awareness, you stand a much better chance of realizing measurable improvements. That is why it's essential to pay close attention to the factors that cause a person to commit to a task, the emotional states of performers during their activities, and the overall motivation and attitude of the performers. Several issues are at work here.

The first is how to create a committed performer. Commitment cannot be mandated or forced. People become committed to a task, an activity, or a goal by choice. Take the father who has decided to coach a youth sports team. He gets no compensation for it, except maybe psychologically. He invests a great deal of time and physical and emotional energy and may not even win one game. Yet he is committed to coaching the kids. This same man may or may not be as committed on the job. Why is there such a discrepancy? What causes these people to become committed, and how can you transfer this energy to the job? Or how can you establish a work environment that allows for this commitment on the job all the time?

In a business setting, people need commitment to the organization, job ownership and pride, and an increase in discretionary effort. Managers are actually looking for employees to deliver the same energy and passion on the job that they do after work in their leisure or recreational activities. When you get this type of energy, motivation, and involvement from your people, you get more positive performance at higher levels, greater productivity, and increased loyalty. Essentially, people are capable of doing more with less, or in less time.

COMMITTED TO COMMITMENT

You hear a great deal about the importance of commitment in the pursuit of excellence and success. Engaged performers must be committed to what they are doing; otherwise, they will not involve all their strengths, talents, and resources in the performance. So the question becomes, How do you get people committed to a task?

In Chapter 4, we talk about strengths and talents and their effect on confidence. Tapping into these innate keys to how someone performs is the first step for a manager. You have to identify a person's strengths and talents and then match those to the tasks. It may be redundant to repeat this commonsense point, but you would be surprised at how many managers mismatch their employees and then wonder why performance suffers. When you match strengths with tasks you build confidence. This extends to the development of *self-efficacy,* the personal belief that you can and will successfully complete a task. The more self-efficacy performers have, the more likely they will be to continue undertaking specific tasks. And as their confidence grows, their commitment to success grows. After all, success breeds success—and the whole host of positive feelings associated with it.

Everyone wants to maintain and sustain those positive feelings and will move heaven and earth to repeat the behaviors that led to those feelings. Someone who finds a perfect match between strengths and required tasks will grow in confidence and become more committed. The more commitment, the greater the engagement. The tie-in is obvious, and it may even seem circular. Yet managers don't spend enough time learning what makes a performer committed to a task.

Here are some suggestions to help you build commitment in your people. Ask them what they are good at and what they like to do. Make certain their work tasks match as closely as possible to their strengths and likes. Provide them with positive feedback on a regular basis when they perform well. (As we've said, the management approach that saying nothing means nothing is wrong, and that feedback is only given when something goes wrong, is totally misguided. No-news-is-good-news does not build commitment. In fact, it creates disengagement.) Involve employees in conversations about their performance. Have them evaluate themselves and make suggestions for improvements, incentives, and rewards.

We had the opportunity to put all these things into practice for a client in what will seem to be a very simple solution to a performance problem. But remember, when you are mired in the problem, the solution is apt to be hard to see even if it may be obvious to an outside observer.

Larry was a top salesman for a health club chain. Every month, he received a plaque identifying him as the top performer. This went on for several months, and Larry's sales continued to grow. Then management got the bright idea that all salespeople were motivated by money and nothing else. So they took away the plaques and started awarding cash bonuses for achieving various sales levels. Some people's sales improved, but Larry's started to drop. And they continued to drop over the next several months. That's when we were called in to coach Larry back to his top-performer status.

After we spoke with management and learned of the correlation between Larry's drop in performance and the implementation of the cash bonuses, we figured Larry might have been one of those salespeople who crave recognition more than money. So we went to Larry and asked him what he thought caused his drop in sales. He said it started when they took away his plaques. Now he couldn't decorate his walls with the visible recognition that he was the top performer. He told us that he really didn't want the extra money; he wanted the recognition. And since he wasn't getting it, he was not as committed as he used to be. In fact, he was becoming so actively disengaged that he was thinking about quitting his job—the job where he was once the top performer.

This loss of commitment stopped him from prospecting, from going after potential members who came into the club but did not buy right away, and from working hard to close sales with the people he did see. He was uncommitted and disengaged. He also was not getting any help or support from his sales manager, which contributed more to his disengagement than senior management realized. (Hint: Without support from a leader, supervisor, or manager, the performer tends to disengage almost automatically.) We knew the answer to the problem immediately.

We went back to management and simply told them to give Larry his plaques back, pointing out that when he gets the visible recognition, he gets more motivated and committed. Basically, he becomes more engaged and performs well. Management could not believe the solution *could be so simple but they agreed to listen to our advice. Two months later, Larry was once again the top salesperson in the company. He was committed, motivated, and emotionally engaged in his job.*

EMOTIONAL INTELLIGENCE AND PERFORMANCE ENHANCEMENT

Emotional intelligence was originally thought of as yet more psychobabble that researchers were trying to carry over to the business world. But research has shown that performers and managers who exhibit high levels of emotional intelligence tend to perform better than their counterparts, are more successful overall, and have more satisfying lives. These results hold true regardless of IQ, education, or upbringing.

When you look at these results from a performance enhancement perspective, it makes tremendous sense. People who have the ability to identify and control their own emotions as well as respond appropriately to the emotional states of others should perform better in a variety of situations. Again, it's clear from sports that players who are overemotional or overaroused tend to make more mistakes, get fatigued faster, and more often than not lose the game. Similar results have occurred in business, where emotional outbursts can cost a sale, a client, or a job. So when the researchers in emotional intelligence announce that it is more important than IQ or technical skills as a predictor of success in business for both men and women, listen carefully.

Psychologists have talked about the relationship between healthy emotional states and human achievement for more than a hundred years. Yet the business world is still stuck in the mechanistic view of man as machine. No thinking or feeling, just doing. Follow these steps in the process. Standardize your inputs so you can provide the outputs. Check your heart and mind at the door. After all, the end of the twentieth century gave us hope that this approach could still work.

When TQM and reengineering hit in the early 1990s, they became so popular that businesses were steamrolled into adopting these practices.

But they were just *fads;* they failed miserably in most companies because both concepts left out the people, their thoughts, their motivations, and their emotions. Reengineering and TQM focused only on business processes, to the exclusion of the people carrying out the processes. No one paid attention to the hearts, minds, and emotions of the people. That was a big mistake, one that companies are still paying for today. Pay attention to the people and their makeup, and you'll get more engaged performers who produce better-than-expected business results.

We have always advised our clients that they need to listen better within their organization, build and nurture better relationships between and among people, and care more about each other. This seems like common sense, but for some, it seems too "female oriented," too soft.

Nonetheless, today's more successful companies focus on participatory management, or what we are calling *engagement.* This is actually based on the concept of emotional intelligence, or what might be better called *emotional competence.* Managers who listen to their employees, involve them in decision making, and communicate with them in an open atmosphere of trust and honesty have higher-performing employees. When managers are emotionally competent, their employees are more engaged and their companies realize significant increases in customer satisfaction and loyalty —and profits. Plus, emotional competence and the awareness of the emotional states of others help salespeople be more effective because they are more in tune with the emotional states that affect their customers' buying decisions. These same skills help customer service representatives provide better service, solve problems more quickly, and increase customer satisfaction levels. In fact, many companies are now implementing emotional competence training programs because they realize the value of having emotionally intelligent and fully engaged employees.

This brings up another point, and that is whether emotions really have a place in the workplace. We are of the opinion that emotions in the workplace are good for business. People put their hearts, minds, and emotions into their community, family, and leisure activities. We call that *passion.* And passion leads to engagement. So allow people to be emotional and passionate at work. Give them the opportunity to become emotionally expressive and emotionally intelligent. Businesses, their customers, their employees, and their employees' families will all realize tremendous benefits.

EXPECT THE BEST

There is a concept that has been around so long, you would think it started at the dawn of time. Some people call it the law of attraction. Others think of it as a law of personal magnetism. While it might sound like a cliché, the law states that you attract what you think about the most. This goes for people, money, lifestyles, things, and more thoughts. So if you have a positive mental attitude, your glass will always be full (or at least half full instead of half empty). If you think about performing at your peak at all times, more often than not you will achieve a high level of performance.

Conversely, if you think about negative things that can happen in your life, then you'll probably view the world as negative.

A traveling salesman knocked on a farmer's door as he was heading to the next town and asked the farmer what type of people he would find in the town up ahead. The farmer asked him what type of people he had found in the town he just left. The salesman told the farmer that the people were very negative and unfriendly and did not want to buy what he was selling. The farmer told him that he could expect to find the same type of people when he got to the next town.

A little later on, another salesman knocked on the farmer's door and asked the same question. The farmer asked the salesman what type of people he had found in the town he just came from. This salesman said the people were very positive, very friendly, and very willing to buy what he was selling. The farmer told him that he could expect to find the same type of people in the town up ahead.

So what is the difference between the two salesmen? Attention, focus, perception. The expectations you have for anything, especially a performance of some kind, will affect what you pay attention to, where you focus your mind and efforts, and how you perceive things. Think about the last time you bought a car. All of a sudden, it seems as if your type of car is the only one that you see on the road. That's because your mind is primed for cars that look like yours, so you expect to see more of them. And now that your expectation has been set, your mind focuses your attention and alerts your perception to become aware of the cars like yours. This works for any major purchase or choice; suddenly the world seems to be full of similar instances.

What all these stories add up to is simple. When you expect the best from yourself, you usually get it. When you expect the best from others, they usually rise to the occasion. It is up to every manager to set the bar high enough to stretch people and to clearly communicate what is expected of them. When this occurs, performance is enhanced. When it does not occur, performance decreases and emotional stress increases.

You must help your performers train their own brains to maximize their gains. Then you will truly help them develop a positive core from which all their future performances will grow. Another simple way you can do this and also motivate them to continue to perform at high levels is to praise them.

OPTIMISM—THE FINAL PIECE OF THE PUZZLE

We've almost got this whole thing put together. If you remember, we started at the beginning talking about how positive psychology is one of the foundational elements of the Positive CORE model. One of the principles of positive psychology is optimism. Optimism is the hope and belief that something good will happen. It relates to finding the silver lining, seeing the glass as always half full, and knowing that somewhere near or inside that huge pile of manure there has to be a pony. You get the idea. Optimism keeps people going, helps them explain away failure as a temporary result produced by external causes, not their own lack of skill. Optimism has been called the biology of hope. It strengthens the mind and the immune system and leads to positive motivations.

Some of these motivations are the desires to achieve, to make friends, to fall in love, to feel safe and secure, and to perform well at whatever you do. It's also better to be more intrinsically motivated (doing something for the sheer joy of doing it) than extrinsically motivated (doing something for rewards). What managers need is a way to identify what motivates a performer and help that person become motivated to perform well.

MAXIMIZING MOTIVATION AND GUARANTEEING IMPROVEMENT

Two of the biggest problems every employer faces today are how to continuously motivate employees and how to achieve ongoing improvements in performance. Companies and managers struggle with both situations, throwing incentive programs and increased benefits packages at the problems but not getting the desired results. That's because the problems are inside the employees, and external controls such as incentives will not always get the job done.

Nonetheless, you can virtually guarantee you will get the job done and achieve higher levels of performance. We have created a tool, a job aid if you will, called the Talent Optimization Performance System (TOPS), to help you identify motivational and performance roadblocks as well as how those same factors can contribute to high performance. Basically, TOPS identifies ten areas of motivation that may be the source of performance strengths or the cause of performance problems. Many of these areas correlate to aspects of the Positive CORE model. The first four areas are the big four of motivation and performance improvement:

- **Competence:** Skills and abilities
- **Confidence:** Belief in oneself
- **Consequences:** Reinforcers for performance

- **Commitment:** Dedication to successfully completing a task

The first set is followed by a supporting set of six:

- **Communication:** How clearly performance expectations are communicated
- **Challenge:** How challenging the task is
- **Conflict:** How much stress or conflict the performers face
- **Culture:** How well the organization promotes and rewards successful performances
- **Control:** How much performers believe they control the outcomes
- **Concentration:** How much attention performers pay to the task and for how long

When performance continues at a high level, as with most top performers, you can be certain that these factors are in play. When performance deteriorates or has never been up to par, you can be sure that it is also due to one or more of these ten motivational categories. It is up to managers and companies to identify the cause of the motivational problem and then develop potential resolutions for it.

For example, if competence is the issue, then more skill training may be necessary, job aids may be required, or a job change may be in order. If the performer lacks confidence, what's needed is a series of performance activities similar to the required performance, at which this person can be successful enough to build confidence and self-esteem. When success is achieved, the positive behaviors and outcomes need reinforcement with praise so that the person will continue to perform well.

When performance standards or expectations are not clearly communicated, the performer has no idea of what constitutes a successful outcome. Or if someone is under so much stress as to be unable to perform, we must find ways to minimize that stress and maximize a positive performance environment.

SOLUTIONS TO ENGAGEMENT-RELATED PERFORMANCE PROBLEMS

The most effective solution to any problem begins with asking the employee's opinion. Too often, managers identify a problem and prescribe the answers. They tell the employee what to do, how to do it, and when it must be done. Then the managers wonder why it either never gets done or does not reach the specified performance level. The reason is simple. The manager, not the employee, owns the solution.

You've seen this situation play out in your own life, especially if you are married. It is one of the gender differences in communication styles between men and women. The woman tells the man that she has a problem and she wants to talk about it. He immediately jumps in with his prescribed solution and tells her how to solve her problem. She doesn't follow his advice, leaving him wondering why she didn't listen to him. It's the same as in the work setting where the manager owned the solution. In this personal setting, the man owned the solution. At no time was the performer (employee, woman) involved in generating the solution.

So always ask employees what their problem is first, and ask them what they propose for a solution. It may be that they do require more training, or that they want to change how they are reinforced for their performance, or that they are getting reinforcements that they don't really want, or that they need more guidance and coaching. Whatever the problem, you can be sure the employee has been thinking about it and the possible solutions for a long time. So, as a manager, ask your employees how they would resolve the issue.

When you do this, you move people toward a state of engagement. True success and high levels of performance occur when employees are fully engaged in their jobs. Recent research by the Gallup organization and the Performance Assessment Network (PAN) support this conclusion about fully engaged employees and high performance. That is where managers and employees must get to in order to be successful. And the way to get there is by paying attention to the ten C's of the TOPS system.

Total engagement means employees own the problem and the solution, feel in total control of their performance behaviors and their outcomes and reinforcers, know the consequences for performance or nonperformance, and have the confidence and skill set to do the job well. Employees who are engaged are completely committed to achieving successful outcomes, both for themselves and for their companies. Employees who are engaged will do whatever it takes to get the job done so that everyone wins. Fully engaged employees will continuously challenge themselves to raise the performance bar.

And isn't that what we want from all our employees?

In addition to the previous list of ten areas to identify for motivation and performance problems and solutions, we also offer a more formal assessment in Exercise 4, with comprehensive lists of interview questions complete with rating scales.

OUR CHALLENGE TO YOU

The engagement challenge is very simple. If you want to virtually guarantee performance improvement and enhancement in almost any situation, use our Talent Optimization Performance System (TOPS) to identify the engagement motivation levels of your people as well as those areas that must be attended to in order to achieve higher levels of performance in all areas of your company.

Exercise 4: THE TALENT OPTIMIZATION PERFORMANCE SYSTEM (TOPS)

This guide to motivational engagement and performance improvement helps the manager serve as a performance coach. Altogether, it includes four parts: two sets of interview questions (Parts 1 and 2) for managers to use with their reports, and rating scales, also in two parts. Each of the ten areas in Part 1 has five questions associated with it. The manager sits with an individual performer and asks these questions, takes notes on the answers, and follows up with additional probing questions tailored to the moment. The purpose of this interview is to engage the performer in a conversation about motivational issues that affect performance, either positively or negatively. The questions in Part 2 are optional, to be used at the manager's discretion. Once this interview is completed, the manager will move on to working with the performer to rate skill sets in each area on a linear scale in Part 3. Finally, the results of those ratings will be graphed in Part 4 to create a visual for both the performer and the manager.

Manager's Interview Questions (Part 1)

Directions: Feel free to adapt these base questions for the interview to fit your situation or organization. You may also want to cut each series from five to three questions if time is short. However, we strongly recommend that you complete the entire series of questions to get the best information possible to help your people improve their performances.

You can also provide these interview questions directly to performers and ask them to respond to each one on paper or electronically. Although this does allow a manager to take more people through the process in a shorter period of time, it also detracts from the nuances of the personal interaction. And, since one of the major elements of Positive CORE is the relationship between managers and performers, we suggest you conduct each interview individually.

COMPETENCE: Having the skills needed to do the job

1. Do you currently have the skills or have you ever had the skills to do this job?

2. What were the outcomes of previous jobs like this one?

3. Do you have similar skills that you can adapt to this job?

4. Can you learn new skills to do this job?

5. How satisfied are you with your current skill level and how satisfied will you be when you increase your skill level?

CONFIDENCE: Having a belief in one's ability to successfully complete a task

1. Do you believe you are capable of successfully completing the job?

2. Have you successfully completed similar jobs in the past?

3. What is your success ratio for jobs like these?

4. How confident are you in your abilities as a performer?

5. How will your self-esteem be affected by the outcome of your performance?

CONSEQUENCES: The effects of rewards and punishments on performance

1. What are the positive consequences (rewards) for doing this job well and the negative consequences (punishments) for doing this job poorly?

2. How much will the consequences influence your current and future performances?

3. How much control do you have over the consequences for your performances?

4. How closely are the consequences tied to the performance outcomes, and which specific consequences would you prefer?

5. What do you regard as the reasons for your performance outcomes?

COMMITMENT: The desire and dedication to perform

1. How much do you want to do this job? How passionate are you about this work?

2. How will you benefit from successfully completing this job?

3. What reinforcement will you receive for successfully completing this job?

4. How did you feel when you successfully completed other jobs like this one?

5. How likely are you to do this job or a similar job again, for the same or an even longer period of time?

Exercise 4: THE TALENT OPTIMIZATION PERFORMANCE SYSTEM (TOPS) continued

COMMUNICATION: The ability to clearly express a point of view

1. Have performance expectations been clearly communicated so that you fully understand the expectations and outcome objectives related to your performance?

2. How often do you feel listened to, and how well do you listen to others?

3. What type of performance feedback is provided to you, and when is it provided?

4. What are the preferred methods of communication in this organization, and how do they match up with your preferred methods of communication?

5. What are the communication problems that exist between men and women, between management and staff, and among staff members, and how can they be resolved?

CULTURE: The beliefs and environment of the organization

1. How does your perception of the organization's culture influence and affect your performance?

2. What changes in the organization's culture will help you be more motivated and improve your performance?

3. How do the organization's mission and values align with your personal mission and values?

4. What are the specific organizational motivators and demotivators?

5. What aspects of the organization's culture convince you that this is the best place for you to do your best work?

CHALLENGE: The degree of difficulty that exists in accomplishing a task

1. How hard or easy is it for you to complete your job?

2. How often do you receive stretch goals for your performances?

3. How often are you challenged physically, emotionally, and mentally to exceed your previous performance levels?

4. How much challenge is built into the way you do your job?

5. What must you learn to do a new job well?

CONFLICT: Unresolved emotional or interpersonal issues

1. What causes stress or conflict in your life?

2. What emotions do you feel when you're involved in a conflict or under stress?

3. How often do you think your life is out of control or out of balance?

4. What do you do to resolve conflict in your life?

5. Would your life be better with no conflict or stress in it or a moderate amount of conflict or stress in it, or do you thrive on constant stress and ongoing conflict?

CONTROL: The amount of control or choice a performer has when performing

1. How much control or choice do you have over your performances?

2. How much certainty and predictability exist when you perform?

3. What are the reasons you give for the outcomes of your performances?

4. How much do you or must you rely on others when you are performing?

5. Do you prefer situations that are cooperative or competitive?

CONCENTRATION: How well focus is maintained during a performance

1. How much difficulty do you have maintaining your focus to successfully complete a task?

2. What distracts you while you are performing a task?

3. What specific thoughts go through your mind when you are performing?

4. What do you remember about times when you performed well?

5. How difficult is it for you to concentrate on one task over a long period of time?

Exercise 4: THE TALENT OPTIMIZATION PERFORMANCE SYSTEM (TOPS) continued

Now that you have completed the initial TOPS interview, you may want to ask a few follow-up questions to help you further identify any performance problems.

Manager's Follow-Up Questions for TOPS (Part 2)

Directions: *These follow-up questions can be asked either as part of the initial interview or as a separate approach following the interview. Again, feel free to change or adapt the questions to fit your situation. You may also decide to skip these follow-up questions and go directly to the rating scales. The choice is yours.*

Problem Identification Questions

1. Do you know what is expected of you?

2. Do you believe that what is expected of you can be achieved by you?

3. Do you understand what to do?

4. Are you capable of doing what you're being asked to do?

5. Are you confident you can do what you're being asked to do?

6. Do you need any help achieving what we ask of you?

7. Do we require too much of you?

8. What problems, if any, do you see in doing what you're being asked to do?

9. What do you expect to receive if you do a good job?

10. What do you expect to get if you perform poorly?

11. Do people who perform well get what they deserve?

12. How do you feel about the way performance is rewarded?

13. What do you feel about the reward system here?

14. How well do we follow through on our commitments to employees?

15. What do you think about the way people are treated here?

16. Are top performers treated differently than average or below-average performers?

17. Has the company delivered on its promises to you in the past?

18. Do you want the rewards and incentives being offered to you?

19. Is there anything that you're getting that you do not want or would rather not have?

20. Is there anything that you're not getting that you do want?

21. Is the job providing you with the challenge and recognition you desire?

22. How much do you enjoy what you're doing?

23. How happy are you with your job?

24. What, specifically, can we do to make your job more satisfying?

25. What do you want to tell me that we have not yet discussed?

Emotion Identification Questions

1. Why do you feel that way?

2. What caused you to have those feelings?

3. What feelings are you having, exactly, in relation to this situation?

4. What thoughts are going through your mind related to this situation?

5. What else can you tell me about the situation that's causing you to feel this way?

6. Can you tell me anything else?

7. Can you be more specific when describing your emotions?

8. How are your feelings affected by the situation?

9. How much in control of your feelings do you think you are?

10. Does the job provide you with more positive feelings or more negative feelings?

Once the interview is completed, it is time to assign some numbers to the response categories. Use the scales in Part 3 to have the performers develop personal ratings on each of ten items, following the ten "C" groupings of the interview questions. Then use the graph in Part 4 to plot each performer's scores.

Exercise 4: THE TALENT OPTIMIZATION PERFORMANCE SYSTEM (TOPS) continued

TOPS Rating Scales (Part 3)

Directions: Circle the number that best represents your response to the question associated with the TOPS factor.

COMPETENCE: Do I have the skills to do this job?

0	1	2	3	4	5	6	7	8	9	10

I do not have the skills.   I have some of the skills.   I have all of the skills.

CONFIDENCE: How confident am I that I can do this job well?

0	1	2	3	4	5	6	7	8	9	10

I am not confident that I can do this job well.   I am somewhat confident that I can do this job well.   I am completely confident that I can do this job well.

CONSEQUENCES: How certain am I that the consequences (reinforcements) will be tied to my performance?

0	1	2	3	4	5	6	7	8	9	10

I am sure consequences will not be tied to my performance.   I don't know whether consequences will be tied to my performance.   I know for a fact that consequences will be tied to my performance.

COMMITMENT: How dedicated am I to performing this job well?

0	1	2	3	4	5	6	7	8	9	10

I have no desire to perform this job well.   I am ambivalent about performing this job well.   I am totally committed to performing this job well.

COMMUNICATION: How well is information communicated in this organization?

0	1	2	3	4	5	6	7	8	9	10

Information is never shared.   Information is shared sporadically.   Information is shared regularly.

CULTURE: How well do the beliefs and values of the organization match my own?

0	1	2	3	4	5	6	7	8	9	10

The organization's beliefs and values do not match my own.

The organization's beliefs and values somewhat match my own.

The organization's beliefs and values completely match my own.

CHALLENGE: How difficult and challenging is my job?

0	1	2	3	4	5	6	7	8	9	10

The job is very easy and does not provide much of a challenge.

The job is not very difficult and provides only a moderate challenge.

The job is very difficult and challenging.

CONFLICT: Do I have unresolved conflicts that I need to address?

0	1	2	3	4	5	6	7	8	9	10

I have no conflicts in my life that I must resolve.

I have some conflict in my life that I must resolve.

I have a lot of conflict in my life that I must resolve.

CONTROL: How much control do I have over my performance?

0	1	2	3	4	5	6	7	8	9	10

I have little or no control over my performance.

I have some control over my performance.

I have complete control over my performance.

CONCENTRATION: How well do I focus my attention while performing?

0	1	2	3	4	5	6	7	8	9	10

I have great difficulty focusing my attention.

I am capable of focusing my attention some of the time.

I always maintain my focus.

Exercise 4: THE TALENT OPTIMIZATION
PERFORMANCE SYSTEM (TOPS) continued

TOPS Profile (Part 4)

Directions: *Plot the ratings to provide yourself and your performer with a visual representation of his or her motivational approach to performance improvement. You will want all the scores to move in a positive direction except for the conflict score. That should move in a negative direction; otherwise, the performer may have a problem.*

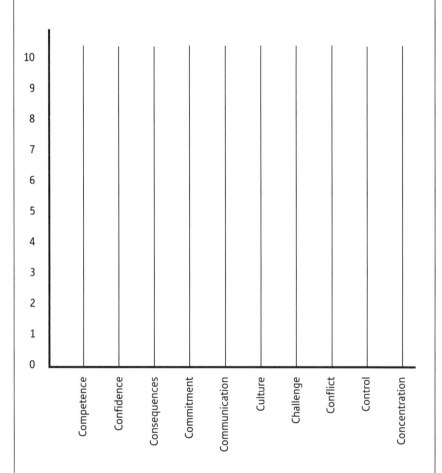

Note: *Once you've identified the performer's motivational strengths, work to match those strengths to the required tasks. This will increase engagement.*

REAL-WORLD
APPLICATIONS

Follow-Up to the CORE

B y taking the Positive CORE approach, you really can help people get better at what they do. In this final chapter, we give you a more in-depth view of how to use Positive CORE at the individual as well as the organizational level.

POSITIVE CORE EXTENSIONS

You can extend Positive CORE from the initial interview stage through practical implementation in three phases. Phase 1 is the interview process that addresses the four competencies of the CORE model, covered in Chapters 4–7. Phases 2 and 3 are extensions of the model that provide a follow-up process to help you help your people be more successful.

During Phase 2, coaching, you meet with your individual performers to review the results of the CORE interview. Implementation, phase 3, is where you and your performer identify who is responsible for what behaviors and how those performances will be measured and evaluated. This final phase of Positive CORE is designed to generate even further commitment to successful outcomes on both your parts.

These follow-up phases do bear some similarity to the standard performance management process. While the concepts may be similar, however, the applications are different. Performance management, from a human resources perspective, will more often than not focus on performance appraisal and what the individual can do to get a better rating in the next appraisal period. The approach in Positive CORE specifically focuses on enhancing the performer's strengths with a minimal focus on weaknesses or areas for improvement. As you already know, a major assumption of the Positive CORE approach is that when you concentrate on a person's strengths and work to enhance them, the weaknesses will naturally be overcome, simply disappear, or visibly improve.

It's worth repeating (after all, repetition is the primary tool for learning and peak performance): this program is designed to identify the CORE elements individuals possess that make them successful. That is, Positive CORE identifies successes and strengths rather than weaknesses and areas for improvement. It involves the target performer or team of performers, their managers, and sometimes all the other stakeholders involved—including family, friends, and colleagues. These interviews are conducted in an effort to determine and describe why performers are where they are, why and how they perform in certain ways at certain levels, and how they accomplish all they do. Remember that success leaves clues. One of the things Positive CORE does for you is uncover those clues.

In addition to the Positive CORE model, some managers find themselves also using the TOPS concept—the Talent Optimization Performance System, introduced in Chapter 7. Whether you use TOPS or not, and we definitely recommend you do, Positive CORE then seeks to take the performer to another level by building effectiveness, productivity, and success in all areas. By helping the performer focus on strengths, we create a multiplier effect so that strengths and successes build on one another. The focus on the positive puts people in a better frame of mind, motivates them even more to continue to achieve, and creates a virtuous cycle of success seeking success. It's as if Positive CORE cycles back on itself and reinforces all the aspects of itself.

CORE INTERVIEWS—PHASE 1

The most comprehensive approach to Positive CORE is to conduct interviews with the individual performer and a series of identified stakeholders who influence, affect, or are affected by the performer. These stakeholders should be the manager of the performer (quite possibly you), co-workers, and possibly even customers. The interviews cover the four areas of Positive CORE: confidence, outcomes, relationships, and engagement. We ask a series of ten to fifteen questions of every interviewee in each of the CORE areas to detect the performer's strengths and how to improve on them. We are looking for commonalities in responses across the entire interview group to determine the perceptions the stakeholders have with regard to the CORE subject's reasons for success. This will help determine how fast, how far, and how high that person can go in the future. The responses are carefully recorded in writing for later review and analysis.

The questions asked of co-workers and the performer are basically the same, with some minor word changes to make them specific for the interviewee. For example, if we ask the performer one of the confidence questions—say, "How confident are you when you are presented with a new task?"—we would change it for a performer's co-worker to read "How confident is [so-and-so] when [he or she] is presented with a new task to complete?" The box on page 166 provides sample questions for the performer that are specific to each of the CORE competencies.

Obviously, the total CORE interview process is more extensive, involving many more questions than the samples in the box. The development of the CORE profile will take quite a bit of time as the interviewer

Sample Interview Questions

Confidence: These questions focus on the performer's beliefs, self-image, self-esteem, skill sets, and commitment to ongoing success, as well as on the consequences the performer receives or achieves for successful or unsuccessful performance.

- How confident are you that you will always do well in whatever you do?
- What are the series of skills you possess that allow you to adapt to different situations?
- How committed are you to continuing your high levels of performance?

Outcomes: These questions focus on the behavioral challenges and obstacles a performer faces in order to achieve specified outcomes, the metrics that are used to measure the levels of achievement and success, including the relevance and meaning of each performance to the performer, and the type of feedback that is provided to link the current performance results to future performance expectations.

- What outcome measures can you create as internal benchmarks?
- How do you measure and evaluate your results?
- How do you receive feedback on your outcomes?

Relationships: These questions focus on the performer's relationships with other people and groups.

- How well do you get along with people you work with? Play with? Socialize with?
- What do you do for other people that no one else does?
- What changes occur in your relationships under stress?

Engagement: These questions focus on how much the performer is engaged in the performance, as well as on the performer's commitment to completing tasks, the emotional aspects of a performance, and the relationship between motivation, optimism, and success.

- What performance expectations do you set that lead to your best results?
- What times of day do you operate at peak efficiency, and how often do you perform your most difficult tasks during your peak operating times?
- How well and how often do you bounce back from adversity, learn from your mistakes, and maintain a positive emotional state?

reads, analyzes, and collates the responses into a cohesive description of the performer. However, the investment of time and energy is worthwhile. Another approach is to modify each of the questions so they can be answered on a 1–10 rating scale, as with the TOPS categories. Even though there is an overlap in one or two TOPS categories with elements of the CORE model (for example, confidence and commitment), the two rating scales can be used separately to provide a more comprehensive picture of the performer's strengths and success clues.

When the individual interviews are completed, you collect, analyze, and categorize the responses. A report is generated for the person to identify strengths, areas for future success, and an overview of the stakeholders' perceptions, attitudes, and beliefs about the person. Then you are ready to move into the next phase, CORE coaching.

COACHING—PHASE 2

Phase 2 of the Positive CORE process is a lengthy meeting with the individual in which all the responses are reviewed, discussed, and evaluated. The process is a time-tested and proven approach to elevating a person to higher levels of success because all participants feel engaged, respected, and appreciated for their involvement and input. We call the main process here the GET RICH Cycle for Personal Success. It has a four-stage process similar to the 4-D process of Appreciative Inquiry (AI): *discover, dream, design, destiny.* We bring up this comparison for two reasons. The first is that more has been published on AI, and readers may be more familiar with those concepts than the concepts of Positive CORE. Also, remember that Positive CORE uses AI as one of its foundational premises, to focus on what an individual already does well. Again, this is done to give the reader a link to information that is already published as we introduce this new approach. It is from this perspective that we created the acronym RICH, which stands for *review, idealize, create,* and *habituate.* Using the process described by this acronym helps a Positive CORE coach, manager, or consultant take the performer through a process that will lead to continued success and consistently higher levels of performance. Basically, we want to help performers exploit what they already do well and find ways to make their performance even better. As one of our clients said during these coaching sessions, "You mean you want to make our peak performance levels the future baseline levels?" And our answer was an emphatic *yes*.

- **Review:** We review the results of the individual's and stakeholders' interviews and discuss the findings openly. The exchange of feedback leads to a consensus on the areas of greatest strength. The objective here is to achieve consistency and agreement between the interviewer and the individual about the CORE strengths.

- **Idealize:** This stage requires the performer to imagine the best possible future. It answers the question about what the performer would do, look like, feel like, and be, given the knowledge that failure was impossible. Help the performer create the ideal world. Techniques such as visualization, creative brainstorming, and image streaming are used to help identify the ideal situation. The CORE coach works with the performer as a facilitator and a guide without influencing the comments or path of the performer.

- **Create:** Here the performer works to develop the steps that will make the ideal situation a reality. Both strategies and tactics are created, along with an action plan for implementation. Additionally, the coach guides the performer to make sure the tactics can definitely be implemented and the goals are realistic enough to be achieved.

- **Habituate:** This final stage describes the repetitive steps the individual will take to make the imagined future a reality. Factors such as repetition and rewards, recognition, reinforcements, and consequences are put in place to ensure the creation of positive performance habits. Furthermore, self-efficacy, self-confidence, and performance mastery are considered worthy skills to develop as part of the performer's repertoire.

The length of time the person spends with the coach during this phase of the program should be between two and four hours. Of course, more time can be spent if necessary or desired. The most effective practices are developed when each stage is given at least an hour to generate content, create acceptance and agreement, and move toward implementation. This investment in time, energy, and effort on the part of both the performer and the coach (quite possibly you, the manager) is well worth it as ever-increasing levels of performance become the daily norm.

IMPLEMENTATION—PHASE 3

The third and final phase of the Positive CORE process involves implementation, which we call R.S.V.P. for Performance Success. This acronym stands for

- **Responsibilities:** Who will do what to ensure ongoing and future success?

- **Success Criteria:** How will success be measured, evaluated, and rewarded?

- **Value:** What value do the new performance behaviors bring to the person's life, organization, and society, and how do they enhance the Positive CORE?

- **Priorities:** What behaviors will be performed or implemented first to achieve positive results?

This phase requires that people be assigned roles and responsibilities, establish goals and objectives, create measurement and evaluation systems, design feedback channels, develop the necessary training requirements, set the performance priorities, and then implement whatever is necessary to make the idealized vision of the individual both a habit and a reality. This is very similar to a traditional tactical coaching session but is divided systematically to focus on each aspect when it will be most useful. Again, we must emphasize that your time investment in all aspects of the Positive CORE model and process will lead to improved performance results.

SECRETS TO SUCCESS

One other thing must be strongly considered. As you go through the Positive CORE process with your top performers, you will begin to uncover some common secrets to their success. Top performers usually can identify their performance patterns of success, especially with a little help from you. These psychological and behavioral performance patterns that lead to high-level results can be learned, modeled, and duplicated by other performers. It is up to you to relate the relevant aspects of each performer's CORE so that they can see what they do similarly well and what they have to enhance to get to the next level. Here's how we've done it in several different settings.

SALES CORE

Let's begin with a negative example, an automobile dealership that called us in to help optimize performance but then chose to ignore our CORE approach. This client had been experiencing flat sales for two years along with significant turnover in the sales team. Additionally, it was on its fourth general sales manager in that same period. Now, turnover is traditionally high in the retail auto industry, but this turnover was excessive. So we were brought in to help solve the problem and to increase sales.

We began by interviewing everyone on the management team to get an overall feel for the culture of the organization, as well as how the management team perceived the company. Was their view mostly positive or mostly negative? The surprising answer was that it was neither. Most managers felt that the owner fluctuated too much in his handling of rewards and consequences, with no process or system in place for either. Managers, as well as sales and service staff, were confused about how well they were doing, what they were doing, and what was expected of them. That's when we began our individual CORE interviews. We started with the sales and service staffs and left the managers for last. We wanted to make sure that our collection and analysis of the staff responses were not tainted in any way by the responses of the managers.

In a nutshell, here is what we learned from the staff: The confidence levels of the majority of the staff were low. They said they were confused and often felt beaten down because of the inconsistencies. They did not know their expected outcomes or how their performances would be measured. This left them with more uncertainty about what and how they should do their jobs. Only a few of the interviewees said they had strong, positive relationships on the job. The majority of the people were simply glad to get the day over with and go home. As for being engaged on the job, many of them laughed at us and the concept. They said they were there for the paycheck and to help the few customers they knew.

We obtained somewhat similar results during interviews with the managers. They did feel more confident than the staff members, however, and their roles and expected performance outcomes were more clearly defined because their bonuses were closely tied to outcomes. Several of the managers hung out together after work. They said that if they had to rate their engagement levels on the job, they would be about a six or seven out of ten. Again, it was not a great atmosphere for promoting top performance.

We created our report and presented it to the owner. We made recommendations on how to increase the CORE of each individual and the organization as a whole. We gave him ideas on how to stop the flood of turnover and to get greater productivity out of his people. We strongly urged him to focus on each person's CORE strengths and attributes and promised that this would lead to higher levels of performance.

He chose to ignore our recommendations and continue on his cur-
rent path. We later learned that he was afraid of losing control over his
staff if he became more positive in his approach, allowed staff members
to identify and play to their strengths, and developed a process of
rewards and consequences based on performance expectations and out-
comes that the staff could identify with and work with. He simply chose
to ignore the CORE and his business continued to slide, turnover con-
tinued to be high, and customer satisfaction continued to drop. We
checked in one more time a few months later and found that even his
service customers, who are usually very loyal to their mechanics, had
started to leave the dealership and drive elsewhere to get their cars serv-
iced. Ignoring the CORE is definitely not good for business.

HEALTH CORE

The emergency room of a regional hospital in Florida began conducting
customer satisfaction exit interviews as part of its new quality initiative.
The goal was to achieve a 92 percent satisfaction rating. For the first year,
that was not a problem as everything was new in the ER, people were
motivated to do their jobs well, and the entire organization was focused
on the quality initiative. However, during the second and third years, customer satisfaction ratings began to decline. When we were called in, exit
interview ratings were down to 82 percent. This 10-percentage-point
decline was definitely not acceptable to the hospital's administration.

We began to investigate the health CORE in the ER by individually
interviewing the doctors, nurses, paramedics, and managers. We also
conducted interviews with ancillary service providers such as patient
transport and radiology staff. We included these two departments in the
interview process because they had the most interaction with ER per-
sonnel and ER patients. It took us several weeks to complete the inter-
view process because of staff schedules and vacations. When it was
finished, we went back to them as a group and had them complete the
TOPS rating scales. We wanted to correlate their perceptions of them-

selves as performers with the qualitative data obtained in the interviews. Here is what we found out.

The nursing staff and the physician staff all thought highly of themselves. Their CORE strengths were quite evident to themselves—but, it turned out, not to each other. Part of the relationship problem in the CORE was that neither department truly respected the skills of the other. This translated into a very mechanical approach to patient care, with nurses behaving respectfully to the doctors in front of patients simply because they were doctors, and for no other reason. They did not have any type of personal or professional friendly relationship with the doctors. And the doctors felt the same way about the nurses. For example, if the telephone was ringing in the ER and all the nurses were busy but a doctor was available to answer it, the doctor refused to answer it because it was "beneath him." Is it any wonder that patient satisfaction ratings were steadily declining?

We set things up so that the doctors and nurses would develop respect for each other's CORE strengths by "walking a mile in each other's shoes." For two hours, doctors performed nursing tasks such as patient triage, taking blood pressure, dressing wounds, and so on. Nurses performed nonsurgical tasks usually reserved to the doctors, such as taking health histories, talking to family members, and conducting basic intake exams. By the end of the session, both departments wanted their old jobs back. The enforced role reversal led them to understand one another at a gut level and realize that they all had to work together and play to their strengths to help the patients.

This change alone helped boost customer satisfaction ratings back up to 90 percent. But that was not enough. So we went to work helping the managers and supervisors do whatever they could to identify the strengths of their team members and then help those people play to their strengths. We had the managers positively reinforce successive approximations of achievement and continuous improvements toward goals. The managers looked for and found ways to enhance the strengths of their team members. We had the ER chief nurse and physician meet with the managers and exchange informal performance reviews of each other's department personnel so that everyone could learn how their co-workers perceived them. We then helped the managers establish realistic performance expectations and outcomes, determine how those performances would be measured and reinforced, and work to build more friendly relationships among all the members of the ER staff. We even helped them establish better communications with the ambulance staff who brought patients to the ER so the entire patient experience would be as positive as possible.

We did a number of things over a two-year period, with the result that customer satisfaction ratings reached a high of 95 percent and averaged 93 percent for three years after we completed our work. The team continued to focus on the CORE of the ER, and it resulted in better patient care, higher satisfaction ratings, and a more collegial environment in which to work, despite the inherent high stress of the ER.

SPORTS CORE

This case study was completed long before we had the idea of Positive CORE, but in retrospect, it was truly a CORE application. It involved a women's college basketball team that Richard was asked to coach for a special exhibition game against a possible Olympic team from Canada.

The regular coach was away on vacation when this exhibition came up, so the school asked Richard to coach the women since he had coached men's high school and college basketball. Richard had two weeks to get the team back in shape, playing together and putting on a respectable show. His first task was to call a team meeting and get to know the players a little better, to find out their true strengths and weaknesses, and to determine who the starting five should be, even if this group turned out to be different from the season's starting five.

One of the things Richard learned was that the team preferred to run instead of playing the sort of slow, methodical game they'd played all season. Since it was just an exhibition game and Richard was the coach, he decided to see if the women could really run during a game. If that was indeed one of their CORE strengths, he would teach them a high-intensity defensive scheme that would allow them to run. During the first week of practice, everyone established goals, defined ways to measure their goals (outcomes), and told Richard what it would take to keep them highly motivated to really put on a top performance during this exhibition. The thing that Richard brought to the practices was that they had to have fun while learning a new way to play.

The team ran during the first several practices. As they continued to play at this up-tempo pace, their mistakes (turnovers) decreased with each successive practice. As their turnovers decreased, their confidence grew. They started to achieve their goals, and then they started to surpass them. The team grew closer (stronger relationships), and everyone became more committed to the cause.

During the second week of practice, Richard implemented a pressing defense and five-person rebounding scheme that forced everyone to run the entire game. He established expectations for them that this type of game plan would cause turnovers for the other team, lead to easy baskets for the home team, and sometimes lead to easy baskets for the other team. He also told the team that they would probably experience a high number of turnovers themselves because of the speed at which they would play. With the outcomes clearly in mind and the expectations realistically set, it was time to see if the team could bring their CORE to the fore. And bring it they did. The team won by twenty-two points, had a tremendous time playing that way, and enjoyed the closer relationships they established. One other thing happened. The coach returned in time for the game and graciously sat on the bench and allowed Richard to coach the entire game without any interference. When she saw the results, she decided to follow the same approach for the following season. She played to the strengths of her athletes instead of her strengths as a coach. She was able to transform herself as a leader for the benefit of the team. The next year, the players, the coach, and the team as a whole all had a winning season.

INDIVIDUAL CORE

Several years ago when Robbie was working as vice president of human resources for a large bank, she inherited a long-term employee who was underperforming as the receptionist. This employee's recent performance evaluations were steadily declining but were not quite at the point where a performance improvement plan or a probationary program had to be implemented. She was close, but not quite there yet. When Robbie went to work every day, she saw an unhappy receptionist going through the motions of answering phones, directing people to offices, and doing trivial work for staff members. Since Robbie was already well versed in the elements of the Positive CORE concept, she decided to apply them to the receptionist.

> *In a series of one-to-one interviews, Robbie learned that the receptionist had very little confidence in her ability to perform this seemingly easy task. The receptionist also was unaware of the outcomes she was supposed to produce or achieve, or how those outcomes would be measured. Because she was grumpy so much of the time, no other employees wanted to spend any more time with her than they had to. And all this had led to the receptionist's "retiring on the job"—withdrawing as much as possible from it. She had little or no motivation and came to work every day simply for the paycheck.*
>
> *By following the CORE model, Robbie was able to find out that the receptionist liked working with numbers and definitely preferred that to working with people. She wanted to do statistical analysis for the human resources department rather than answer phones and direct people to offices. She wanted to manage projects and make her contribution that way instead of being out front, as she called it. Basically, she told Robbie that she was shy and introverted and preferred to work alone to get her job done.*

The solution to this performance problem seems so easy in hindsight. Robbie decided that she would give the receptionist what she wanted and see if she could become a top performer. First, Robbie hired a receptionist with an outgoing personality, a pleasing voice, and a friendly demeanor. This proved to be a great hire as the receptionist job played directly into this person's CORE strengths. Next, Robbie moved the original receptionist to a back-office job where she could work on HR statistics, develop reports, and manage projects without having to interact with large numbers of people. This seemed likely to play to her strengths. The result was nothing short of amazing.

Within two months, the former receptionist's attitude and behavior had changed for the better. She came to work with a smile and even said hello to people. She got all her work done on time, soon required very little supervision, and produced work worthy of a top performer. Robbie's performance evaluation of her was quite different from the previous supervisor's. While once disengaged, unconfident, and lonely, the employee was now a highly motivated, extremely confident team player. Although she still preferred to work alone, she felt she was part of the HR team because her analyses, reports, and projects all contributed to the success of the department.

OUR CHALLENGE TO YOU

We leave you with several challenges. The first is to learn as much as you can about your own strengths, what lights your fire, and what you do to be a top performer. Then do the same for everyone who works with you and for you.

Next, take the Positive CORE model and display it in your workplace. Teach your people about it: the concepts, how they work with each other, and how you will strive to find and maximize the strengths of everyone on your team.

Before you have to give someone a poor performance evaluation, ask yourself if they are using their CORE strengths. Ask yourself if they are a good match for the job they are doing, or if their CORE strengths lie elsewhere. If they have other strengths, move them to a job where they will excel.

Finally, in a bit of positive selfishness, we want you to combine the CORE with the TOPS model when you work with your people. Play to and enhance their strengths. Improve the areas that are near but not quite strengths and ignore the weaknesses—just leave them behind. You'll have to be very confident to do this, but we know you can. Challenge your people to be the best they can be, to find and exhibit their CORE. And then sit back, relax, and watch performance and productivity soar.

INDEX

(